SILVERSTONE
SHADOWS

Dedicated to the memory of
Ken and Norah Tyrrell

SILVERSTONE SHADOWS

Closer to the action in the 80s & 90s

Foreword by Nigel Mansell

BRYAN APPS

HALSGROVE

First published in Great Britain in 2010

British Library Cataloguing-in-Publication Data
A CIP record for this title is available from the British Library

ISBN 978 0 85704 062 6

HALSGROVE
Halsgrove House,
Ryelands Industrial Estate,
Bagley Road, Wellington, Somerset TA21 9PZ
Tel: 01823 653777   Fax: 01823 216796
email: sales@halsgrove.com

Part of the Halsgrove group of companies
Information on all Halsgrove titles is available at: www.halsgrove.com

Printed and bound in China by Toppan Leefung Printing Ltd

CONTENTS

The author is indebted to
Bob Tyrrell, Nigel Mansell, Murray Walker,
Autosport, Motor Sport *and* F1 Racing.

Nigel Mansell, 1985.

FOREWORD BY NIGEL MANSELL OBE

THE BRITISH GRAND PRIX has always had a special place in the hearts of British motor racing enthusiasts, and this has been even more the case since it became the only occasion in the course of the year when all the Formula 1 teams could be seen in action in this country.

Silverstone has grown immeasurably in stature since 1948 when, as a thinly disguised Battle of Britain airfield, it staged the first race to be given that title for the cars and drivers who had survived the war. I am delighted that, after many years of uncertainty, the future of the circuit is now assured.

The British Grand Prix crowds occupy a unique place in the hearts of the British drivers who, like me, are ranked amongst its winners. Of all the events in the calendar it is the one they most want to win because, in spite of the noise of the cars and the insulating effect of the helmets, they can feel the enthusiasm of the crowd which is worth a second a lap to them.

Each of my four wins was important to me because each had to be fought for and won. 1986 was especially memorable because, after my car had failed only seconds after the start, events conspired to place me in the spare Williams Honda with which I was able to win the race after all. Bryan briefly describes the course of all thirteen races and also lists the starting grid positions and the results in full. His previously unpublished photographs, taken from his privileged position within the paddock and the pits, succeed in conveying the very special atmosphere of these occasions. They also offer a record of the cars and the people associated with them.

This book is also a tribute to Ken Tyrrell who, having seen Jackie Stewart win three World Championships with his cars in the early years, pressed on with undiminished enthusiasm when the economic circumstances were against him.

Since the very first painting he sent me in 1985 Bryan has offered me unstinting encouragement and support and I am delighted to be associated with this book.

Nigel Mansell OBE
2010

1985 FIA FORMULA ONE
WORLD CHAMPIONSHIP

TYRRELL

HOLDER OF PASS NO I ....011081...

BRITISH GP 1985

THE HOLDER OF THIS CREDENTIAL MUST BE
GIVEN FREE ACCESS AT ALL TIMES INTO THE
CIRCUIT AND AREAS DESIGNATED BELOW.

TRACK

PADDOCK

PADDOCK

1986 FIA FORMULA ONE
WORLD CHAMPIONSHIP

FOCA

HOLDER OF PASS NO. ....02331....

BRITISH GP 86

THE HOLDER OF THIS CREDENTIAL
MUST BE GIVEN FREE ACCESS AT ALL
TIMES INTO THE AREAS
DESIGNATED.

FRI	SAT	SUN
1	2	3

ADMISSION

FIA
FORMULA 1
WORLD
CHAMPIONSHIP
GUEST
ADMIT TO
PADDOCK
ONLY
ISSUED TO:
TYRRELL
PASS NO.
431737

FRI	SAT	SUN
1	2	3

BRITISH G.P. 1989

NEARER THE HEAT
OF THE ACTION

MY FIRST PADDOCK PASS was given to me by Raymond Mays who was known as the "father" of the B.R.M. It was in 1953 when I was sixteen and he had written to say that if I showed his letter to someone at the entrance to the paddock at Goodwood that Easter Monday I would be taken to meet him. It didn't happen because my father insisted that we should set off for home before the last race to avoid the traffic, and that was a massive disappointment. However I did have the opportunity that day to watch Reg Parnell and Ken Wharton drive the fabulous V16 BRMs in the Chichester Cup and the Glover Trophy races, and I met Raymond Mays thirty years later at Bourne in Lincolnshire where he was able to show me all the BRMs at close hand.

In 1985 I was invited to write a book based on some scrapbooks I had compiled in the 1950s about the BRMs and I thought that a day at Silverstone during the weekend of the British Grand Prix would be an ideal opportunity to take a look at the contemporary motor racing scene at close hand. I wrote to Ken Tyrrell asking him how I might go about watching the practice on Friday and, to my surprise and delight, he sent me one of his Tyrrell paddock passes. It enabled me both to meet Ken and to photograph all the Formula 1 cars at close quarters in the paddock, the pits and the pit lane. In 1986 Bernie Ecclestone very generously sent me a paddock pass for the British Grand Prix at Brands Hatch, saying that it would enable me to get "nearer the heat of the action", and in the years that followed, right up until he sold the Tyrrell Racing Organisation in 1998, Ken never failed to send me a paddock pass for the Friday Practice before the British Grand Prix at Silverstone. It was a great privilege to have access to the pits and the paddock over all those years and to record with my camera everything that caught my eye. Above all, it was an enormous pleasure to come to know Ken and Norah and to enjoy their friendship and hospitality in the company of their drivers and other members of the team in their pits and motor home.

Ken Tyrrell was a towering figure in the motor racing world of his day. His cars enabled Jackie Stewart to win the World Drivers' Championship in 1969, 1971 and 1973 and yet his enthusiastic involvement with motor racing never stifled his interest in football and cricket. When his cars were racing overseas he would ask Fleet Street reporters if they knew how Spurs were doing, and when Jackie Stewart brought his Tyrrell-Ford into the pits in pouring rain during practice at the Nurburgring to complain about the conditions and the problems with his car Ken bent down to him and shouted, "You think you've got problems. England are 86 for six!" In the 80s and 90s the Tyrrell team lacked the financial resources of its chief rivals but nevertheless managed to punch above its weight, with Ken drawing upon some brilliant designers and engineers. In 1990 Jean Alesi gloriously led the United States and Monaco Grands Prix for many laps with Harvey Postlethwaite's revolutionary 019 Tyrrell Ford. In 1998 the 026

Tyrrells had a much more advanced and powerful V10 Ford engine but Ken Tyrrell had retired and so the team's real driving force had gone.

There was a special relationship in the 1980s and 1990s between the British Grand Prix, Silverstone, the crowd and Nigel Mansell which has been best expressed by Murray Walker in *F1 Racing* magazine. "From the old BBC commentary position in the Dunlop Tower, which commanded a view of much of the circuit, I was privileged to talk about so many great races, many of them with the incomparable James Hunt by my side as we sometimes almost literally wrestled with each other for the sole microphone. And who gave me the greatest pleasure during those wonderful years? Without a doubt it was Our Nige, 'Il Leone', Nigel Mansell. His brilliant fighting comeback in 1987 to catch and defeat his abrasive team mate Nelson Piquet was one of the greatest races I've ever seen and the annual Mansell-mania of his devoted fans who caused Silverstone to bulge at its seams, willing him to win, always made the atmosphere absolutely electric. To this day there's no crowd like a Silverstone crowd for knowledgeable enthusiasm and passion."

The years 1985 to 1997 were memorable in the annals of the British Grand Prix. They witnessed four spectacular wins by Nigel Mansell, and one each by Damon Hill and Johnny Herbert, but those bare facts don't begin to tell the story of the excitement and drama of the thirteen races. I will attempt to do that in this book with the aid of the many photographs I took from the paddock and the pits.

THE 1985 BRITISH GRAND PRIX

SILVERSTONE JULY 19 20 21

"Prost Perfect" – *Autosport*

1985

BRITISH GRAND PRIX

Starting Grid

1. **K. Rosberg** Williams Honda
   1 min 05.591 secs
2. **N. Piquet** Brabham BMW
   1 min 06.249 secs
3. **A. Prost** McLaren TAG
   1 min 06.308 secs
4. **A. Senna** Lotus Renault
   1 min 06.324 secs
5. **N. Mansell** Williams Honda
   1 min 06.675 secs
6. **A. Alboreto** Ferrari
   1 min 06.793 secs
7. **A. de Cesaris** Ligier Renault
   1 min 07.448 secs
8. **E. de Angelis** Lotus Renault
   1 min 07.581 secs
9. **T. Fabi** Toleman Hart
   1 min 07.678 secs
10. **N. Lauda** McLaren TAG
    1 min 07.743 secs
11. **S. Johansson** Ferrari
    1 min 07.887 secs
12. **D. Warwick** Renault
    1 min 08.238 secs
13. **P. Tambay** Renault
    1 min 08.240 secs
14. **R. Patrese** Alfa Romeo
    1 min 08.384 secs
15. **M. Surer** Brabham BMW
    1 min 08.587 secs
16. **J. Laffite** Ligier Renault
    1 min 08.656 secs
17. **G. Berger** Arrows BMW
    1 min 08.672 secs
18. **M. Winkelhock** RAM Hart
    1 min 09.114 secs
19. **T. Boutsen** Arrows BMW
    1 min 09.131 secs
20. **M. Brundle** Tyrrell Renault
    1 min 09.242 secs
21. **P. Alliot** RAM Hart
    1 min 09.609 secs
22. **E. Cheever** Alfa Romeo
    1 min 10.345 secs
23. **P. Martini** Minardi Motori Moderni
    1 min13.645 secs
24. **J. Palmer** Zakspeed
    1 min 13.713 secs
25. **P. Ghinzani** Osella Alfa Romeo
    1 min 16.400 secs
26. **S. Bellof** Tyrrell Ford Cosworth
    1 min 16.596 secs

I ARRIVED AT SILVERSTONE early on Friday morning in torrential rain but my paddock pass worked its magic and I soon crossed over the footbridge to enter the hallowed ground of the paddock. Within the welcome shelter of the Tyrrell pits two mechanics were watching over the new 014 Tyrrell Renault, which was designed by Maurice Phillipe and would be driven by Martin Brundle, and the earlier 012B Tyrrell Ford Cosworth car which had been assigned to the rising German star Stefan Bellof. My presence was cordially accepted within the pits by the two mechanics who were joined by others and the two drivers before Ken Tyrrell arrived to give me a hearty welcome. The noise of the engines being warmed up within the confines of the pits was painful until ear-plugs came to my aid, and I proceeded to photograph everything I saw. Ken later crossed to the pit wall between the pit lane and the circuit to watch the cars as they screamed by at high speed and he invited me to join him. The Press was particularly interested in the prospect of Martin Brundle driving the first turbo-engined Tyrrell but, over coffee in his motor home, Ken told me that Tyrrell was only fourth in line for Renault engines and his didn't have the performance of those with which Renault had favoured the Lotus team. He was enthusiastic about Stefan Bellof whom he said would be another Jackie Stewart. Over lunch I sat with Norah Tyrrell and we were again joined by Ken.

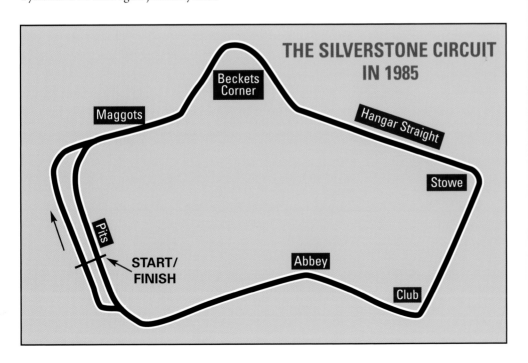

THE SILVERSTONE CIRCUIT IN 1985

Beckets Corner

Maggots

Hangar Straight

Stowe

Pits

START/ FINISH

Abbey

Club

British Grand Prix

Results
1. **Prost** McLaren
   MP4 TAG V6 turbo
2. **Alboreto**
   Ferrari 156 V6 turbo
3. **Laffite** Ligier
   JS25 Renault V6 turbo
4. **Piquet** Brabham
   BT54 BMW S4 turbo
5. **Warwick** Renault
   RE60B V6 turbo
6. **Surer** Brabham
   BT54 BMW S4 turbo
7. **Brundle** Tyrrell
   014 Renault V6 turbo
8. **Berger** Arrows
   A8 BMW S4 turbo
9. **Patrese** Alfa Romeo
   V8 turbo
10. **Senna** Lotus
   97T Renault V6 turbo
11. **Bellof** Tyrrell
   012B Ford V8

**The following failed
to finish:**
Lauda McLaren
   BP4 TAG V6 turbo
Boutsen Arrows
   A8 BMW S4 turbo
De Cesaris Ligier
   JS25 Renault V6 turbo
Martini Minardi M185
   Motori/Modoerni V6 turbo
De Angelis Lotus
   97T Renault V6 turbo
Winkelhock RAM
   03 Hart S4 turbo
Rosberg Williams
   FW10 Honda V6 turbo
Mansell Williams
   FW10 Honda V6 turbo
Cheever Alfa Romeo
   185T V8 turbo
Palmer Zakspeed
   841 S4 turbo
Fabi Toleman
   TG185T Hart S4 turbo
Johansson Ferrari
   156 V6 turbo
Tambay Renault
   RE60B V6 turbo
Alliot RAM 03 Hart
   S4 turbo
Ghinzani Osella-Alfa Romeo

Winner's average speed:
146.274 mph

The unofficial practice session was abandoned, as the low dense clouds had caused the airstrip to be closed, delaying the arrival of the rescue helicopter which would have been essential in transporting casualties to hospital in the event of a major accident. Eventually an untimed session of just twenty minutes was allowed with a ten minute break before the official timed practice began. While everyone waited in the rain for things to start happening, the Lotus mechanics provided some unscheduled entertainment by racing two JPS liveried Sinclair C5s in the pit lane. I came upon Jonathan Palmer who appeared to be trying to coax his Zakspeed to fire on all its cylinders in the paddock behind the pits.

When the practice was finally underway Martin Brundle complained that he couldn't get all of the 900 bhp of his Renault engine on to the track, and he brought the car in for a quick check after spinning at Woodcote. Stefan Belloff discovered that his tyres were unsuited to the only normally aspirated car in the race. He would do much better when he drove the turbo car in the German Grand Prix on 4 August. In 1985, when fuel was strictly limited and mid race refuelling not allowed, the drivers of turbo cars had to be sparing with their use of their boost, or risk running out of fuel.

Keke Rosberg was fastest in his Williams Honda on both Friday and Saturday, and Prost's McLaren, with its TAG sponsored Porsche engine, was alongside him on the starting grid on Sunday afternoon. Brundle and Bellof were 20th and 26th, but when the field went off on its formation lap, Brundle's car stalled and so he was forced to line up at the very back of the grid.

The race: 65 laps of 2.93 miles circuit

At the start of the race Senna's Lotus Renault came up from fourth place on the grid to lead into Copse and the order at the end of the first lap behind Senna was the two Williams Hondas of Rosberg and Mansell, and the McLaren TAG of Prost. Four cars were eliminated by a multiple collision further down the field while Cheever's Alfa Romeo climbed from 22nd place to 11th place. Senna's lead continued to increase and both he and Rosberg began to draw away from all the others while, at the same time, they kept watchful eyes on their fuel consumption. Prost was overtaken by the Ligier Renault of de Cesaris but then regained his position, while de Angelis lost a whole half an hour in the pits with his Lotus Renault. Having failed to find anything wrong with its engine they discovered that it performed perfectly when they eventually started it up again! Mansell retired from fifth place with a failed clutch and soon afterwards Rosberg had to abandon the race with a blown turbo. Meanwhile Prost was catching Senna while Lauda snatched third place from de Cesaris in his McLaren TAG. The two leading cars seemed to have the race to themselves when, with twelve laps to go, Senna's car developed an intermittent misfire which enabled Prost to get past him on lap 57. Lauda's McLaren TAG slowed just as Prost was about to lap him and this allowed Senna to pass both Prost and Lauda in one go, but Prost soon resumed his place at the front when Senna's engine began to falter once more. Prost went on to win and was unchallenged at the end after Senna's car coasted to a stop on lap 60 out of fuel, being classified 10th after the race. It was a cruel misfortune after such a splendid performance. Alboreto was a distant second in his Ferrari and Laffite third in the Ligier Renault.

Martin Brundle finished 7th after a steady race in the Tyrrell Renault from last place on the grid while Bellof came 11th in the non-turbo car.

Alain Prost, who was known as "the Professor" for his cerebral approach to racing, became the first Frenchman to become a World Champion racing driver at the end of the 1985 Season. Having won the British Grand Prix at Silverstone convincingly, *Autosport*'s headline comment was, "Prost Perfect!"

Writing later of the first Tyrrell Renault, Martin Brundle told me, "I am afraid it's a car which I have had a love-hate relationship with. It hasn't been the best of cars to drive, frightening me silly on several occasions, but at the same time it did get me to the finish line at many Grands Prix."

Before Friday's practice in the Tyrrell, Renault, McLaren and Ferrari pits.

The Tyrrell 014 with a Renault V6 turbo engine in the Silverstone pits early on Friday morning.

The Tyrrell 012 with a Ford Cosworth DFY V8 engine in a still-deserted pits.

Derek Warwick's Renault V6 turbo receiving some early morning attention. He would come from twelfth place on the grid to finish fifth in the race.

Then current World Champion
Niki Lauda's McLaren TAG
bearing the number 1.

Stefan Johansson's Ferrari
with his distinctive helmet
conveniently placed in its
side pod.

The Ferrari transporter with the famous rampant horse prominently displayed. It was the squadron badge of Francesco Baracca, the Italian hero of the First World War and his father Count Enrico Baracca had asked Enzo Ferrari to display it on all his cars.

The great Ayrton Senna standing by the side of his JPS Lotus transporter. In his book *Grand Prix Heros*, Murray Walker summed him up as "unique and unforgettable".

A McLaren TAG with Nicki Lauda's Number 1 parked next to the McLaren transporter. A close inspection suggests that it is not the car that he used in the race.

Above: Martin Brundle setting out in the 014 Tyrrell Renault in which he would start from the back of the grid and finish 7th. He gave me a key ring with an image of his helmet.

Below: With no reverse gear Formula 1 cars had to be pushed back into the pits after a practice run.

The rising star Stefan Bellof, regarded by Ken as a future Jackie Stewart, chatting to a friend in front of the Tyrrell pits before the untimed practice began. He was killed at Spa on 1 September in a sports car race.

The Tyrrell Ford being driven away from the pits by Bellof. He finished in 11th place in the race.

Stefan Bellof returning to the pits.

Alain Prost, "the Professor," in the McLaren TAG. 3rd in practice, fastest in the warm pp, he would win the race on Sunday.

Niki Lauda, who retired on lap 57 with electrical problems. World Champion in 1975,1977 and 1984, he survived a horrific accident in 1976.

Michele Alboreto whose Ferrari would be 6th in practice and finish 2nd in the race. He achieved Tyrrell`s last Grand Prix win in 1983 and was killed while testing in Germany in 2001.

Keke Rosberg, 1982 World Champion. After gaining pole position with his Williams Honda he retired on lap 21 with turbo failure.

Nigel Mansell's "Red 5" Williams Honda. 5th in practice, he retired on lap 19 with clutch problems.

Ayrton Senna's JPS Lotus Renault which was 4th in practice but retired on lap 60 when his car ran out of fuel.

Top left: Elio de Angelis in his JPS Lotus Renault. He was 8th in practice but only completed 37 laps of the race. He was killed while testing at Paul Ricard in 1986.

Top right: Nelson Piquet in the Brabham BMW. 2nd in practice and 4th in the race, he was World Champion in 1981 and 1983 with Bernie Ecclestone`s Brabham team.

Philippe Alliot's RAM Hart. 21st in practice, he was eliminated by an accident on the first lap of the race.

Teo Fabi's Toleman Hart. Senna was prevented from winning the Monaco Grand Prix in a Toleman in 1984 when the race was stopped because of heavy rain. The team was to become renamed by Benetton.

Jacques Laffite's Ligier Renault which was 16th in practice and finished 3rd in the race.

Riccardo Patrese's Alfa Romeo caused excitement when its turbo exploded. This was the last Alfa Romeo to compete in Formula 1.

Receiving attention. Patresse was 14th in practice and finished 9th after completing 62 laps of the race. Cheever's Alfa retired on lap 17 with engine trouble.

THE 1986 BRITISH GRAND PRIX

BRANDS HATCH JULY 11 12 13

"Mansell's Brands Triumph" – Motor Sport

THE PADDOCK PASS THAT Bernie Ecclestone had sent me covered all three days and so I decided to go to Brands Hatch on the Sunday to watch the race itself. Arriving early I chanced to meet Nigel Mansell in the paddock and so was delighted to have the opportunity to offer him my best wishes for the race. In spite of his recent serious road accident, Frank Williams was able to be there to watch Nelson Piquet claim pole position and Nigel Mansell, who had troubles with his car in practice and who everyone had come to see win the race, complete the front row of the grid. I was also able to meet Ken Tyrrell again and he told me that he was pleased that Bernie had "fixed me up with a pass."

Only turbo-engined cars were eligible to race in 1986 and the two 015 Tyrrell Renaults of Martin Brundle and Phillippe Streiff were lighter and more robust than the previous year's car. The development of the new cars had been seriously delayed by a number of major accidents earlier in the year and, after Phillippe Strieffs' car spun on Friday afternoon, aerodynamic changes were hastily made overnight. The two were 11th and 16th on the starting grid. Ayrton Senna whose Lotus had the very latest EF15C Renault engine was 3rd in practice, behind the two Williams Hondas. Nelson Piquet had a spectacular blaze from his turbo during the warm up on Sunday morning but the mechanics were able to prepare it for the race without recourse to the spare car.

There was a festive atmosphere before the race as everyone eagerly looked forward to the start. In the course of an air show, a vast Vulcan bomber flew unbelievably low over my head so that it seemed temporarily to blank out the sky! The good natured crowd of 150,000 enthusiasts appeared to be crammed into every square inch of ground around the sun-drenched circuit.

The race: 75 laps of the 2.614 mile circuit

At the start of the race Mansell was the quickest away from the line but, as I watched in dismay, his car suddenly slowed down going into paddock bend with what turned out to be a broken half shaft coupling which limited its power to only one wheel. His race was over before it had begun, but almost immediately, so was the race itself as a multiple collision occurred behind him! Poor Jacques Laffitte had to be flown by helicopter to Sidcup Hospital with badly injured legs and when the race was eventually restarted, at 6 minutes past four, Mansell had the good fortune to be able to resume his place on the grid alongside Piquet in the spare Williams Honda.

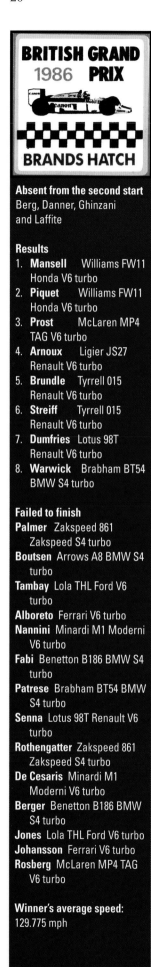

Absent from the second start
Berg, Danner, Ghinzani
and Laffite

Results
1. **Mansell**   Williams FW11
    Honda V6 turbo
2. **Piquet**   Williams FW11
    Honda V6 turbo
3. **Prost**   McLaren MP4
    TAG V6 turbo
4. **Arnoux**   Ligier JS27
    Renault V6 turbo
5. **Brundle**   Tyrrell 015
    Renault V6 turbo
6. **Streiff**   Tyrrell 015
    Renault V6 turbo
7. **Dumfries**   Lotus 98T
    Renault V6 turbo
8. **Warwick**   Brabham BT54
    BMW S4 turbo

Failed to finish
Palmer   Zakspeed 861
    Zakspeed S4 turbo
Boutsen   Arrows A8 BMW S4
    turbo
Tambay   Lola THL Ford V6
    turbo
Alboreto   Ferrari V6 turbo
Nannini   Minardi M1 Moderni
    V6 turbo
Fabi   Benetton B186 BMW S4
    turbo
Patrese   Brabham BT54 BMW
    S4 turbo
Senna   Lotus 98T Renault V6
    turbo
Rothengatter   Zakspeed 861
    Zakspeed S4 turbo
De Cesaris   Minardi M1
    Moderni V6 turbo
Berger   Benetton B186 BMW
    S4 turbo
Jones   Lola THL Ford V6 turbo
Johansson   Ferrari V6 turbo
Rosberg   McLaren MP4 TAG
    V6 turbo

Winner's average speed:
129.775 mph

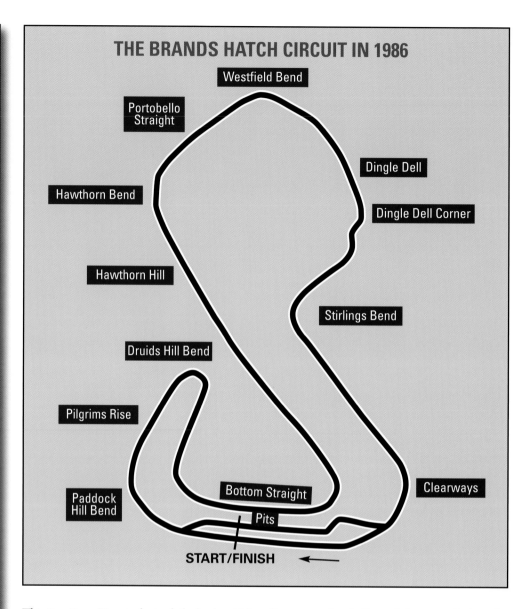

This time it was Piquet who took the lead and Mansell was overtaken by Berger's Benetton BMW as he accustomed himself to the strange car. He reclaimed second place on lap three, 1.7 seconds behind Piquet and then, with typical grit and determination, set the fastest lap of the race up to that point before taking the lead on lap 23. Senna retired in his Lotus Renault with a broken gearbox on lap 28 and Mansell was closely pursued by Piquet who in turn was followed by Alboreto's Ferrari, Arnoux's Ligier Renault and Warwick's Brabham BMW. Piquet came in for new tyres on lap 30, being stationary for 9.04 seconds and two laps later Mansell followed suit with a time of 9.57. Nigel exited the pit lane and entered Paddock Bend fractionally before his team mate arrived and Piquet managed momentarily to draw alongside him. There were no team orders and the two cars circulated nose to tail as everyone held their breath and a banner appeared in the crowd expressing the popular sentiment: "GIVE 'EM HELL NIGEL." The atmosphere on that summer's afternoon was unforgettable with everyone waving and cheering Nigel on as the two Williams Hondas repeatedly lowered the lap record. Both cars lapped Prost's McLaren TAG which was in third place! After seventy laps Piquet finally became reconciled to coming second and dropped back. They finished the race in that order with Arnoux fourth behind Prost and the Tyrrell Renaults of Brundle and Streiff fifth and sixth. Johnny Dumfries was seventh in the second Lotus Renault. No one had thought to put a water bottle in the spare Williams Honda and consequently Nigel was suffering from dehydration. It was an extraordinary performance and a hugely popular win. Nigel told me later that Nelson had missed one gear during the whole race and that had cost him the lead.

Stefan Johansson's Ferrari in the darkened pits with the sunlit grandstands beyond. He was 18th in practice and retired on lap 20 when a stone punctured his radiator.

Nelson Piquet's William's Honda in the pits. He was fastest in practice and finished 2nd to Nigel Mansell in the race.

The Williams Honda engine covers were removed to allow adjustments to be made.

McLaren TAG nose sections
present and correct.

The scene behind the
McLaren pits.

Nigel Mansell immediately before the race.

Nigel Mansell signing race programmes for some of his many fans.

The V6 turbo Honda engine of the all-conquering Williams exposed.

Gerhard Berger's Benetton
BMW, the successor to the
Toleman Hart.

Relaxing in the McLaren
motor home.

The clock ticks on towards
the start.

Yet more tyres? Behind the
Tyrrell pits.

Above: Consternation in the pits at news of the multiple crash.

Below: Nelson Piquet leads Nigel Mansell after the second start.

Nigel Mansell beginning to close on Nelson Piquet with Ayrton Senna's JPS Lotus Renault tailing them.

Nigel Mansell's crucial pit stop.

Derek Warwick's pit stop.

Michele Alboreto retires in his Ferrari on lap 51.

THE 1987 BRITISH GRAND PRIX

SILVERSTONE JULY 10 11 12

"People Power" – Autosport

Starting Grid

1. **N. Piquet** Williams Honda
   1 min 07.110 secs
2. **N. Mansell** Williams Honda
   1 min 07.180 secs
3. **A. Senna** Lotus Honda
   1 min 08.181 secs
4. **A. Prost** McLaren TAG
   1 min 08.577 secs
5. **T. Boutsen** Benetton Ford
   1 min 08.972 secs
6. **T. Fabi** Benetton Ford
   1 min 09.246 secs
7. **M. Alboreto** Ferrari
   1 min 09.274 secs
8. **G. Berger** Ferrari
   1 min 09.408 secs
9. **A. de Cesaris** Brabham BMW
   1 min 09.475 secs
10. **S. Johansson** McLaren TAG
    1 min 09.541 secs
11. **R. Patrese** Brabham BMW
    1 min 10.012 secs
12. **S. Nakajima** Lotus Honda
    1 min 10.619 secs
13. **D. Warwick** Arrows Megatron
    1 min 10.654 secs
14. **E. Cheever** Arrows Megatron
    1 min 11.053 secs
15. **A. Nannini** Minardi Moderni
    1 min 12.293 secs
16. **R. Arnoux** Ligier Megatron
    1 min 12.402 secs
17. **M. Brundle** Zakspeed
    1 min 12.632 secs
18. **C. Danner** Zakspeed
    1 min 13.337 secs
19. **A. Campos** Minardi Moderni
    1 min 13.793 secs
20. **A. Caffi** Osella Alfa Romeo
    1 min 15.558 secs
21. **P. Alliot** Lola Ford
    1 min 15.868 secs
22. **P. Streiff** Tyrrell Ford
    1 min 16.524 secs
23. **J. Palmer** Tyrrell Ford
    1 min 16.644 secs
24. **I. Capelli** March Ford
    1 min 16.692 secs
25. **P. Fabre** AGS Ford
    1 min 18.237

IT WAS GREAT TO MEET up again with Ken and Norah Tyrrell in 1987 and also to renew my acquaintance with the Silverstone paddock and pits. For 1987 both turbo and normally aspirated cars were eligible, the non-turbo engines having been increased from 3 to 3.5 litres, and the cars, while competing with the rest, were also placed in a category of their own. The new 016 Tyrrells, designed by Brian Lisles, were powered by V8 Ford Cosworth engines. In the course of the year Jonathan Palmer would win the Jim Clark Cup for the drivers of non-turbo cars and both he and Philippe Streiff would together win the Colin Chapman Trophy for the constructors. Other major teams, such as Williams and Lotus, continued to field turbo-engined cars. The Tyrrells were now sponsored by Data General and, as always, their gleaming body panels were assiduously sprayed with a liquid polish and buffed up the moment they so much as paused in the pits. When I crossed the footbridge to buy more rolls of film for my camera I was amazed to see the crowds of people who lined the wire mesh perimeter fence hoping to get a glimpse of the drivers. One in particular seemed to be confident that I would give him my pass!

During the Friday practice both Ayrton Senna and Michele Alboreto signed some paintings I had brought along especially for the purpose. Nelson Piquet gained pole position in practice once again in his Williams Honda but his team mate, Nigel Mansell, whose car had spun dramatically after incurring a puncture, was only 0.07ths of a second slower. Ayrton Senna was third fastest with his Lotus Honda now in bright yellow Camel colours, and Alain Prost's McLaren TAG was third. Streiff and Palmer were 22nd and 23rd.

The race: 65 laps of the 2.969 mile circuit

At the start Prost got past Mansell and Piquet to head the field into Copse but Piquet retook the lead before the second bend and Mansell, using less wing than Piquet, was soon in second place. The two Williams Hondas then proceeded to pull away from the field.

Berger's Ferrari, Arnoux's Ligier Megatron and de Caesaris' Brabham BMW had all retired when Mansell suddenly experienced a slight vibration caused by a balance weight dropping off his front left wheel. It had been intended that both Williams Hondas would cover the entire race on their original sets of Goodyear tyres, but Mansell was losing ground and so he was forced to come into the pits on lap 35, approaching half distance. He was stationary for 9.54 seconds while all four wheels were changed. Commenting on the race James Hunt said that Piquet's driving had improved since the Press had compared him unfavourably to Mansell, but in spite of that the gap between Piquet and Mansell, which had been increased by the pit stop from 1 to 28 seconds steadily narrowed as Nigel, now with fresh

Shell Oils

BRITISH GRAND PRIX

SILVERSTONE 12TH JULY 1987

Results
1. **Mansell** Williams FW11B Honda V6 turbo
2. **Piquet** Williams FW11B Honda V6 turbo
3. **Senna** Lotus 99T Honda V6 turbo
4. **Nakajima** Lotus 99T Honda V6 turbo
5. **Warwick** Arrows A10 Megatron S4 turbo
6. **Fabi** Benetton B187 Ford Cosworth V8
7. **Boutsen** Benetton B187 Ford Cosworth V8
8. **Palmer** Tyrrell 016 Ford Cosworth V8
9. **Fabre** AGS JH22 Ford Cosworth V8

Failed to finish
Streiff Tyrrell 016 Ford Cosworth V8
Brundle Zakspeed 871 Zakspeed S4 turbo
Prost McLaren MP4 TAG V6 turbo
Alboreto Ferrari V6 turbo
Cheever Arrows A10 Megatron S4 turbo
Campos Minardi M186 Moderni V6 turbo
Caffi Osella FA1 Alfa Romeo V8 turbo
Danner Zakspeed 871 Zakspeed S4 turbo
Patrese Brabham BT56 BMW S4 turbo
Johansson McLaren MP4 TAG V6 turbo
Nannini Minardi M186 Moderni V6 turbo
De Cesaris Brabham BT56 BMW S4 turbo
Berger Ferrari V6 turbo
Alliot Lola LC87 Ford Cosworth V8
Arnoux Ligier JS29C Megatron V6 turbo
Capelli March 871 Ford Cosworth V8

Winner's average speed
146.208 mph

tyres, put on a storming performance that thrilled the crowd. The Williams pit crew signalled "TYRES OK" to Piquet, indicating that he could stay out on his original set, but Murray Walker intoned, "Chasing, chasing, chasing" as Nigel steadily shortened the distance between himself and the leader, reducing the lap record in the course of an inspired drive. At 48 laps the difference was 11.45 seconds and Piquet's tyres were beginning to lose their grip. Alain Prost coasted to a stop, the 10th retirement in the race, and "GO NIGE GO" was held out by someone in the crowd which waved and shouted, as one, right around the circuit. Mansell was aware of this enthusiastic encouragement as he drove on the limit to the end. Senna and Prost were lapped by the flying Williams Hondas and on the 63rd lap the inevitable happened as Nigel performed his famous "Silverstone two step move," tricking Piquet into making room for him coming down Hanger Straight so that he could drive down the inside at Stowe Corner. In this way Mansell recorded one of his most notable wins and, unknown to the crowd, his fuel gauge had registered empty for the last two laps of the race. When he was forced to stop on the slowing down lap he was engulfed by his admiring fans.

Jonathan Palmer was first of the non-turbo cars and eighth overall, while Philippe Steiff's Tyrrell had retired on lap 57 with engine trouble.

A Williams transporter in the paddock.

'Red 5' looking resplendent in the paddock.

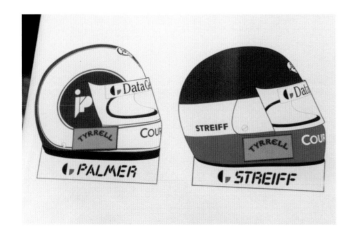

Top left: The Tyrrell drivers' helmets.

Top right: The Tyrrell transporter.

Above left: The McLaren transporter.

Above right: The Ferrari transporter.

Left: The Lotus Honda transporter now in yellow.

Below: The view from the pit wall with the circuit on the right.

Jonathan Palmer's 016 Tyrrell Ford minus its wheels. He would be 23rd in practice and finish the race 8th, the first of all the normally-aspirated cars.

White on shining black from an 016 Tyrrell Ford.

Above: Mechanics working at the front end of one of the Ferraris.

Below: A discussion taking place around Alboreto's Ferrari.

Ferrari's Michele Alboreto making a point.

Riccardo Patrese's Brabham BMW off duty in the pits.

Lotus body-covers lined up in front of the pits.

Benetton's colourful engine cover.

Above: A Benetton receiving attention at the front end.

Below: Thierry Boutsen in the multi-coloured Benetton Ford. He was 5th fastest in practice and came 7th in the race.

Roger Hill (facing the camera) was Tyrrell's Chief Mechanic from 1968 to 1998.

Philippe Streiff's Tyrrell back again in the pits.

Brian Lisles, Tyrrell's chief designer in 1987 nearest the car on the right.

Nigel Mansell driving down the pit lane to join the circuit in his Williams Honda. 2nd fastest in practice, he would win the race.

Ayrton Senna in his Lotus Honda in Camel yellow but with cigarette manufacturer's brand name banned at Silverstone. He was 3rd in practice and 3rd in the race.

Ivan Capelli in his March Ford which was on the last row of the starting grid in 24th place and retired on lap 3 with gearbox problems.

Andrea de Cesaris in his Brabham BMW. 9th in practice, he retired on lap 8 after a broken fuel pipe set fire to his car.

Derek Warwick in his Arrows Megatron. He was 13th fastest in practice and finished in 5th place in the race.

THE 1988 BRITISH GRAND PRIX

SILVERSTONE JULY 10 11 12

"Senna: Master in the Wet" – Motor Sport

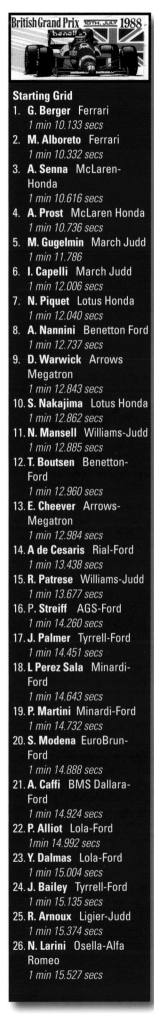

IT WAS HIGHLY UNLIKELY that Nigel Mansell would add to his wins when he came to Silverstone in 1988 as his Williams was powered by a normally-aspirated Judd engine. Ayrton Senna had joined Alain Prost in driving one of the turbo-charged McLaren Hondas but this formidable team, unusually in 1988, lined up in the second row of the starting grid behind the two Ferraris of Gerhard Berger and Michele Alboreto. Ayrton Senna had spun twice in practice while Alain Prost complained of handling problems, and all this led to the abandonment of the recent modifications to improve the airflow over the McLarens. Derek Warwick, in the Arrows Megatron, was the fastest of the British drivers in practice and, to the dismay of Nigel Mansell's many fans, he was right down in 11th place after sliding off the circuit on Friday when his computer controlled 'reactive suspension' behaved unpredictably. Fortunately Patrick Head finally agreed to his request to revert to a conventional suspension for the race. Also to Nigel's advantage, heavy rain on Sunday reduced the power advantage of the turbo-engined cars. The March Judds of Mauricio Gugelmin and Ivan Capelli surprised everyone by occupying the third row of the starting grid. Later in the year Robin Herd invited me to visit his remarkable March team at Bicester.

The 017 Tyrrells Fords, black but with a splash of yellow added as a result of their Camel sponsorship, were driven by Julian Bailey and Jonathan Palmer, but there were problems relating to their seat mountings on Friday and also with the rev counter on Palmer's car. Both drivers complained of a lack of front-end grip. Palmer was 17th and Bailey 24th on the grid.

The race: 65 laps of the 2.969 mile circuit

At the start of the race the two Ferraris of Berger and Alboreto led off the line but Senna, always superb in the rain, passed Alboreto on the first lap and then set about chasing Berger while Prost, who in contrast was never happy in the rain, made a poor start and was only 11th at the end of the first lap. The leading trio left the rest of the field behind but it was not until lap 15 that Senna chose to go past the leading Ferrari when he and Berger were about to lap Prost's McLaren Honda! The Ferrari drivers were concerned about their fuel consumption and so allowed Senna to draw away from them, while Nannini in his Benetton Ford, together with Mansell and Gugelmin, was also closing on the two Italian cars. On lap 20 Mansell, who excels whether it be wet or fine, and even more when he is at Silverstone, overtook Nannini and passed Alboreto to run in third place two laps later. Prost decided to withdraw from the race altogether on lap 24 as he was so far back and thought it was pointless to continue in the atrocious conditions. Eventually the track began to dry and Mansell, went out of his way to find puddles with which to cool his tyres and this enabled Nannini, in taking a more economical line, briefly to re pass

Results

1. **Senna** McLaren MP4
   Honda V6
2. **Mansell** Williams FW12
   Judd V8
3. **Nannini** Benetton B188
   Ford Cosworth DFR
4. **Gugelmin** March 881
   Judd V8
5. **Piquet** Lotus 100T
   Honda V6
6. **Warwick** Arrows A1B
   BMW Megatron
7. **Cheever** Arrows A1B
   BMW Megatron
8. **Patrese** Williams FW12
   Judd V8
9. **Berger** Ferrari F1/87-88C
10. **Nakajima** Lotus 100T
    Honda V6
11. **Caffi** BMS Dallara Ford
    Cosworth DFZ
12. **Modena** EuroBrun ER188
    Ford Cosworth DFZ
13. **Dalmas** Lola LC88 Ford
    Cosworth DFZ
14. **Alliot** Lola LC88 Ford
    Cosworth DFZ
15. **Martini** Minardi M188
    Ford Ford Cosworth DFZ
16. **Bailey** Tyrrell 017
    FordCosworth DFZ
17. **Alboreto** Ferrari F1/
    87-88C
18. **Arnoux** Ligier JS31
    Judd V8
19. **Larini** Osella FA1L Alfa
    Romeo V8

Failed to finish
Boutsen Benetton B188
   Ford Cosworth DFR
Capelli March 881 Judd V8
Prost McLaren MP4
   Honda V6
Palmer Tyrrell 017 Ford
   Cosworth DFZ
De Cesaris Rial ARC1 Ford
   Cosworth DFZ
Streiff AGS JH23 Ford
   Cosworth DFZ
Sala Minardi M188 Ford
   Cosworth DFZ

Winner's average speed
124.142 mph

him. It was to no avail because the Benetton Ford spun at Woodcote on the next lap, making the order Senna, Berger and Mansell. Nigel was now benefitting from the care he had taken of his tyres earlier in the race and passed Berger on lap 50 to the delight of the crowd, having at one stage been as much as fifty seconds behind him. He was clearly enjoying himself in a car which, for once in 1988, he felt he could drive with confidence. Berger was suffering from a shortage of fuel and dropped back to ninth place by the end of the race. Senna's lead was such that he could afford to ease back to save fuel as he reeled off the remaining laps of the race and he was followed across the finishing line by Mansell, Nannini and Gugelmin. Julian Bailey was 16th two laps behind the winner while Jonathan Palmer had retired on lap 14 with transmission trouble.

The crowd had been treated to a superlative display by the rain master Ayrton Senna but, in commenting upon Mansell's spirited drive to second place, Murray Walker rightly said "the crowd was seeing what it had come to see".

Above: The Larrouse transporter.

Right: The Coloni transporter.

Below left: The Benetton transporter.

Below right: The Arrows transporter.

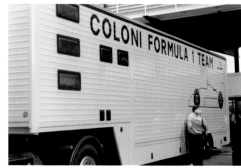

The scene behind the pits.

The footbridge from the paddock across the circuit.

Julian Bailey being helped into his 017 Tyrrell Ford.

Jonathan Palmer before
setting out in his Tyrrell.

Ken Tyrrell with chief designer
Brian Lisles.

Ken Tyrrell with Team
Manager Rupert Manwaring.

Ken Tyrrell in typical good humour.

Both Tyrrells being prepared for action.

Julian Bailey about to set out for another practice run.

Ayrton Senna's McLaren
Honda, 3rd in practice and the
winner of the race.

Derek Warwick's Arrows
Megatron with its tyre
warmers still in place. He
was 9th in practice and
finished 6th in the race.

Above: Alessandro Nannini's Benetton Ford was 8th in practice and finished 3rd in the race.

Below: Ivan Capelli in his March Judd which was 6th in practice and retired with a faulty alternator on lap 34.

Above: Rene Arnoux's Ligier Judd which was 25th in practice and finished the race 18th and three laps behind the winner.

Below: Alain Prost who had an unhappy race in his McLaren Honda. 4th in practice, he withdrew on lap 24 when lying in 16th position.

Above: Nelson Piquet's Lotus Honda which was 7th in practice and finished in 5th place in the race.

Below: Philippe Alliot's Larrouse Lola Ford, 22nd in practice and 14th in the race.

Piquet and Senna out on the circuit while a Ligier Renault heads for the pits.

Philippe Streiff's AGS Ford which retired on lap 8 after a spin having been 16th in practice.

THE 1989 BRITISH GRAND PRIX

SILVERSTONE JULY 14 15 16

"Advantage Prost" – *Autosport*

THE ERA OF THE 1.5 TURBO engine which began with Renault back in 1977 came to an end in 1989 as turbos were banned from the beginning of the season. Nigel Mansell had left Williams at the end of the previous year and signed to drive for Ferrari. He wrote to me from Italy in January to say that he was into "the new year, new team and new car and plenty of pasta!" In March he gave the John Barnard-designed car its first win in Brazil, and was immediately dubbed 'il leone' by the tifosi.

At Silverstone Nigel's Ferrari was third in practice to the more powerful but less manageable McLaren Hondas of Ayrton Senna and Alain Prost and the crowd was encouraged to hope for another Mansell win when he posted the fastest lap in the warm up on Sunday morning.

Ken Tyrrell had two 017 cars at Silverstone as the new 018 models, designed by Harvey Postlethwaite, were not yet ready. These would be the first Tyrrells to be entirely designed on computers without the use of any drawing boards. Michele Alboreto had returned to the team briefly but a conflict existed between his sponsorship by Marlboro and Tyrrell's by Camel and this resulted in his place being taken by Jean Alesi. Jean was described by Murray Walker as "the mercurial French Sicilian" and he would fully justify that description in 1990. Ken introduced me to Jean in the pits against a wall of sound from his car's engine as it was being held at high revs by a mechanic. A form of sign language became necessary as Ken told him that I was a priest and that, if he got on my right side, I would put a word in for him with the "Man Up There!" Over lunch Norah reminisced about the glory days when Jackie Stewart had won World Championships with the Tyrrell team and she had worked the stop watches. Both Tyrrell drivers had a troubled practice, Alesi being delayed with a gear box failure, and adjustments had to be made overnight to improve the set ups of both cars. Palmer's fast lap on Saturday was spoilt by an insect flying into his helmet at speed. Palmer was 18th in practice and Alesi was 22nd. Radical steps had been taken before the race to cure a problem with the McLaren Hondas' oil tanks and Ron Dennis was satisfied that they had been successful.

The race: 64 laps of the 2.969 mile circuit

At the start of the race on Sunday the McLaren Hondas of Prost and Senna led out of Copse Corner with the Ferraris of Mansell and Berger immediately behind them in third and fourth places. Then Senna overtook Prost, the two cars more than once coming dangerously close to a collision which would surely have eliminated them both. After four laps Berger's car began to develop a misfire and, after losing five minutes in the pits on lap 4 with a metering unit problem, he eventually retired on lap 49 when his gearbox failed. Difficulties relating to Senna's new transverse gearbox caused him to come perilously close to

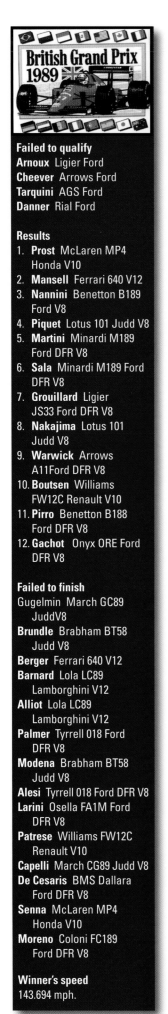

British Grand Prix 1989

Failed to qualify
Arnoux Ligier Ford
Cheever Arrows Ford
Tarquini AGS Ford
Danner Rial Ford

Results
1. **Prost** McLaren MP4
   Honda V10
2. **Mansell** Ferrari 640 V12
3. **Nannini** Benetton B189
   Ford V8
4. **Piquet** Lotus 101 Judd V8
5. **Martini** Minardi M189
   Ford DFR V8
6. **Sala** Minardi M189 Ford
   DFR V8
7. **Grouillard** Ligier
   JS33 Ford DFR V8
8. **Nakajima** Lotus 101
   Judd V8
9. **Warwick** Arrows
   A11Ford DFR V8
10. **Boutsen** Williams
    FW12C Renault V10
11. **Pirro** Benetton B188
    Ford DFR V8
12. **Gachot** Onyx ORE Ford
    DFR V8

Failed to finish
Gugelmin March GC89
   JuddV8
Brundle Brabham BT58
   Judd V8
Berger Ferrari 640 V12
Barnard Lola LC89
   Lamborghini V12
Alliot Lola LC89
   Lamborghini V12
Palmer Tyrrell 018 Ford
   DFR V8
Modena Brabham BT58
   Judd V8
Alesi Tyrrell 018 Ford DFR V8
Larini Osella FA1M Ford
   DFR V8
Patrese Williams FW12C
   Renault V10
Capelli March CG89 Judd V8
De Cesaris BMS Dallara
   Ford DFR V8
Senna McLaren MP4
   Honda V10
Moreno Coloni FC189
   Ford DFR V8

Winner's speed
143.694 mph.

spinning several times as he motored at top speed and his McLaren finally dug itself into the gravel at Becketts on lap 12. The partisan crowd rejoiced at his misfortune as did his team mate Prost. Alesi moved rapidly up the field in the opening laps in his Tyrrell Ford to 10th place on the twelfth lap. Way ahead of him Alain Prost continued to lead only narrowly from Mansell who drove magnificently and brought the Silverstone crowd to its feet, eager to see the red car win. Meanwhile the Williams Renaults of Tiery Boutsen and Riccardo Patrese were lying third and fourth a good way behind, but on lap 20 Patrese, having overtaken Boutsen, spun out of the race at Club Corner. Prost's lead over Mansell remained slender and Jean Alesi moved up to sixth place which he held until his Tyrrell Ford spun and stalled as he attempted to pass Alliot's Lola Lamborghini. Palmer also spun and retired on lap 32 as he came out of Stowe while trying to cope with his car's handling problems and shed at least one wheel in the process.

On lap 43 Nigel Mansell's Ferrari slowed with a puncture in its right front Goodyear and he was a whole minute behind the leader after he had limped back to the pits with a rapidly disintegrating tyre and been equipped with a set of replacements. This led Prost to decide that he had time to stop for new tyres on lap 47 but he then found that he was delayed for 25 seconds when a wheel stubbornly refused to come free. This gave hope to the crowd as the gap between the first two cars was reduced to 12 seconds with 17 laps to go. Mansell was urged on right around the circuit but the there was no real prospect of the Ferrari making up the deficit. He registered the fastest lap of the race but Prost was 19 seconds ahead of him at the end. Alessandro Nannini's spirited drive to third place with the Benetton Ford, in the teeth of opposition from Williams, Lotus and March, enlivened the race behind the leaders.

The Leyton House March transporter.

The Minardi transporter.

Above: Nelson Piquet's Lotus Judd in the paddock.

Below: and in the pit lane.

Jean Alesi in a pensive mood.

Helmeted and ready to go.

Alesi surrounded by cameras as he prepares to leave the pits.

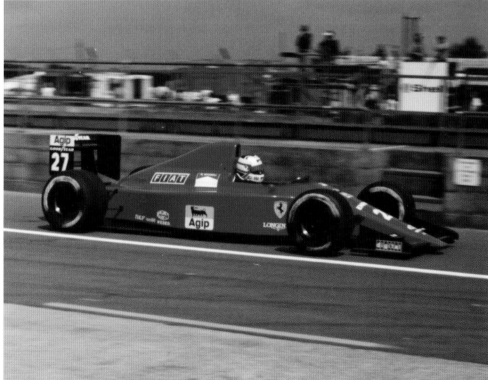

Nigel Mansell, now driving a Ferrari, passing the Tyrrell pits. He was 3rd in practice and finished 2nd in the race.

Above: Ayrton Senna's McLaren Honda in which he was fastest in practice but eliminated from the race after going into the gravel on lap 11.

Below: Alain Prost who won the 1989 British Grand Prix in his McLaren Honda after being 2nd in practice.

Emanuel Pirro in his Benetton Ford which started from the back row of the grid and finished in 11th place.

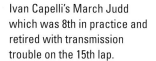

Ivan Capelli's March Judd which was 8th in practice and retired with transmission trouble on the 15th lap.

Yannick Dalmas in the AGS Ford which failed to qualify for the race.

Pierluigi Martini in the Minardi
Ford which was 11th in
practice and finished 5th
in the race.

Robert Moreno in the Coloni
Ford which was 14th in
practice but retired on lap 2
with gearbox trouble.

THE 1990 BRITISH GRAND PRIX

SILVERSTONE

"Hat-trick of Grand Prix wins" – *Motor Sport*

ARRIVING EARLY ON FRIDAY morning I was particularly looking forward to meeting Jean Alesi again and to seeing the 019 Tyrrell Ford with which he had so spectacularly led both the Phoenix and Monaco Grands Prix earlier in the year. In staying ahead of Ayrton Senna's McLaren Honda at Monaco he had managed to throw his car around the narrow street circuit in a way that had beggared belief. The new Tyrrell was designed by Harvey Postlethwaite who, with the aerodynamicist Jean-Claude Migeot, had devised the car's revolutionary raised nose and anhedral wing which would soon become the norm in Formula 1. Its Cosworth Ford engine had been prepared by Brian Hart. It was also good to see the return of 'Tyrrell blue' on the cars, the transporter of course having been repainted to match. Incredibly Alesi was second fastest on Silverstone's power circuit on Saturday morning and sixth on the starting grid. Satoru Nakajima was twelfth. But the real hero of the hour on Saturday afternoon had to be Nigel Mansell who secured pole position for Ferrari, leaving the McLaren Hondas of Ayrton Senna and Gerhard Berger in second and third places.

The race: 64 laps of the 2.969 mile circuit

At 2 00pm on Sunday afternoon it was Senna who flew away at the start of the race, followed by Mansell and Berger. Prost was sixth and Alesi seventh. Piquet had started from the back of the grid with his Benetton Ford after stalling his engine before the formation lap, but he stormed through the field in the early laps to get amongst the top ten. Alesi came into the pits on lap 10 having worn out his tyres in his enthusiasm, and he dropped back to seventeenth place after changing the old ones for new. In the meantime Mansell was shadowing Senna and waiting for his moment to pass. They were often literally nose to tail and at one point Mansell actually got his car alongside but, after what had been a truly epic dual, Senna uncharacteristically spun on lap 14 coming out of Copse and allowed Mansell easy access. Soon afterwards, Senna pitted for a new set of tyres which dropped him to tenth place. His McLaren Honda was suffering from oversteer but he managed to claw his way back into third place by the end of the race though this was in part through the retirement of others. The crowd cruelly rejoiced at Senna's misfortune and cheered Nigel on as he appeared to be enjoying a secure lead from Berger while Prost was third. Then, on lap 22, Mansell's gearbox suddenly became unpredictable, occasionally selecting a gear of its own choice, and as a result of this Berger was soon past the crippled Ferrari to take the lead. After this the problem with Mansell's gearbox seemed to resolve itself and both Mansell and his team mate Prost went past the McLaren on lap 28. Capelli was going great guns at this stage in his Leyton House Judd and also managed to overtake Berger to lap in third place behind the two Ferraris. Sadly the crowd was moved to groan again as the problem with Mansell's gearbox returned and Prost, who had been content to finish second to his team mate, was obliged to take the lead himself on

Results
1. **Prost** Ferrari 641 V12
2. **Boutsen** Williams FW13B Renault V10
3. **Senna** McLaren MP4 Honda V10
4. **Bernard** Lola 90 Lamborghini V12
5. **Piquet** Benetton B190 Ford V8
6. **Suzuki** Lola 90 Lamborghini V12
7. **Caffi** Arrows A11 Ford DFR V8
8. **Alesi** Tyrrell 019 Ford DFR V8
9. **Modena** Brabham BT59 Judd V8
10. **Larini** Ligier JS33B Ford DFR V8
11. **Pirro** Dallara BMS190 Ford DFR V8
12. **Barilla** Minardi M190 Ford DFR V8

Failed to finish
Alliot Ligier JS33B Ford DFR V8
Berger McLaren MP4 Honda V10
Mansell Ferrari 641 V12
Capelli Leyton House March CG901 Judd V8
Donnelly Lotus 102 Lamborghini V12
Warwick Lotus 102 Lamborghini V12
Tarquini AGS JH25 Ford DFR V8
Alboreto Arrows A11 Ford DFR V8
Patrese Williams FW13B Renault V10
Nakajima Tyrrell 019 Ford DFR V8
Nannini Benetton B190 Ford V8
De Cesaris Dallara BMS190 Ford DFR V8
Martini Minardi M190 Ford DFR V8

Failed to start
Gugelmin Leyton House March CG90 Judd V8

Winner's average speed
145.253 mph

lap 43. Berger then dropped back through the field until he retired on lap 60 with a broken throttle. On lap 56, after enjoying a short spell in which his car seemed to acquire greater momentum once more, it was all over for Nigel, and he parked up on the grass no longer able to transmit any power to his wheels. Capelli had also retired as had Berger, and it was in this way that Senna inherited third place behind Prost's Ferrari and Tiery Boutsen's McLaren Honda. Of the Tyrrell Fords, Jean Alesi finished in 8th place one lap down, while Sartoru Nakajima had retired on lap 20 with electrical problems. It was the third win in a row for Alain Prost and, as the disappointed fans made their way home, Nigel Mansell, who had thrown his gloves into the crowd, announced that he would retire from motor racing at the end of the season.

Above left: Jean Alesi
receiving an encouraging
hand.

Above right: Satoru Nakajima
relaxing in the pits.

Satoru Nakajima's 019 Tyrrell
Ford being pushed back into
the pits after a number of
high speed practice laps.

Jean Alesi returning with the
Tyrrell Ford with which he had
impressed everyone at
Phoenix and Monaco. The
car's revolutionary raised
nose and anhedral wing
is clearly visible.

Alesi's car being
reversed into its pit.

Above: Alain Prost's race-winning car in the Ferrari pits.

Below: Nigel Mansell in conversation in the Ferrari pits.

Nigel Mansell passing the Tyrrell pits at some speed in his Ferrari with which he would be fastest on practice but retire on lap 55 of the race with a defective gearbox.

Ayrton Senna in his McLaren
Honda which was 2nd in
practice and 3rd in the race.

Riccardo Patrese in the
Williams Renault which was
7th in practice but eliminated
from the race on lap 26 after
being shunted by Alessandro
Nannini.

THE 1991
BRITISH GRAND PRIX
SILVERSTONE JULY 12 13 14

"Mansell Mania!" – *Autosport*

1991 13th-14th JULY
British Grand Prix

Starting Grid
1. **N. Mansell** Williams Renault
   1 min 20.939 secs
2. **A. Senna** McLaren Honda
   1 min 21.618 secs
3. **R. Patrese** Williams Renault
   1min 22.109 secs
4. **G. Berger** McLaren Honda
   1 min 22.476 secs
5. **A. Prost** Ferrari
   1 min 22.478 secs
6. **J. Alesi** Ferrari
   1 min 22.881 secs
7. **R. Moreno** Benetton Ford
   1 min 23.265 secs
8. **N. Piquet** Benetton Ford
   1 min 23.626 secs
9. **M. Gugelmin** Leyton House March
   1 min 24.044 secs
10. **S. Modena** Tyrrell Honda
    1 min 24.069 secs
11. **J.J. Lehto** Dallara Judd
    1 min 24.141 secs
12. **M. Blundell** Brabham Yamaha
    1 min 24.165 secs
13. **A. de Cesaris** Jordan Ford
    1 min 24.169 secs
14. **M. Brundle** Brabham Yamaha
    1 min 24.345 secs
15. **S. Nakajima** Tyrrell Honda
    1 min 24.560 secs
16. **I Capelli** Leyton House March
    1 min 24.587 secs
17. **B. Gachot** Jordan Ford
    1 min 24.592 secs
18. **E. Pirro** Dallara Judd
    1 min 24.654 secs
19. **T.Boutsen** Ligier Lamborghini
    1 min 25.174 secs
20. **G. Morbidelli** Minardi Ford
    1 min 25.222 secs
21. **E. Bernard** Lola Ford
    1 min 25.537 secs
22. **A. Suzuki** Lola Ford
    1 min 25.583 secs
23. **P. Martini** Minardi Ford
    1 min 25.583 secs
24. **J. Herbert** Lotus Judd
    1 min 25.689 secs
25. **M. Hakkinen** Lotus Judd
    1 min 25.872 secs
26. **M. Alboreto** Footwork Hart
    1 min 26.192 secs

B EFORE THE BRITISH GRAND Prix in 1991 the Silverstone circuit had been radically revised with the introduction of new or revised corners which reduced average speeds while increasing its overall length. In spite of his announcement to retire the previous year, Nigel Mansell was now back with Williams and this time with a V10 Renault engine at his back, and he heartily approved of the changes for which Tom Walkinshaw was largely responsible, as did most of the drivers. He had recently won the French Grand Prix at Magny-Cours.

One of the first things I did when I arrived at Silverstone on Friday morning was to seek out the Jordan pits. Earlier in the year I had sent a painting to Eddie Jordan of Jordan Ford and this prompted Ken Tyrrell to say, tongue in cheek, "He needs your prayers!" This was Jordan's first year in Formula 1 and Michael Schumacher's sparkling performance in the car later in the year brought him a seat in the

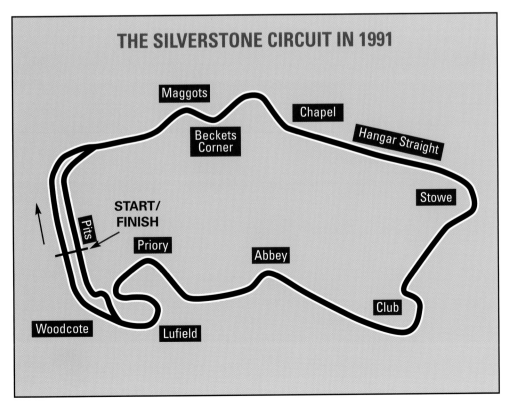

THE SILVERSTONE CIRCUIT IN 1991

Maggots

Chapel

Beckets Corner

Hangar Straight

Stowe

START/ FINISH

Pits

Priory

Abbey

Club

Woodcote

Lufield

Results

1. **Mansell** Williams FW14
Renault V10
2. **Berger** McLaren MP4
Honda V12
3. **Prost** Ferrari 643 V12
4. **Senna** McLaren MP4
Honda V12
5. **Piquet** Benetton B191
Ford HB V8
6. **Gachot** Jordan 191
Ford HB V8
7. **Modena** Tyrrell 020
Honda V10
8. **Nakajima** Tyrrell 020
Honda V10
9. **Martini** Minardi M191
Ferrari V12
10. **Pirro** Dallara B191
Judd V8
11. **Morbidelli** Minardi M191
Ferrari V12
12. **Hakkinen** Lotus 102B
Judd V8
13. **Lehto** Dallara B191
Judd V8
14. **Herbert** Lotus 102B
Judd V8

Failed to finish
Blundell Brabham
BT60Y Yamaha V12
De Cesaris Jordan 191
Hart HB V8
Alesi Ferrari 643 V12
Suzuki Lola 91 Hart DFR V8
Boutsen Ligier JS35B
Lamborghini V12
Brundle Brabham BT60Y
Yamaha V12
Alboreto Footwork FA12
Hart DFR V8
Gugelmin Leyton House
March CG911 Ilmor V10
Moreno Benetton 191
Ford HB V8
Bernard Lola 91 Ford
DFR V8
Capelli Leyton House
Marach CG911 Ilmor V10
Patrese Williams FW14
Renault V10

Winner's average speed
131.227 mph

Benetton team. When I found Eddie in the Jordan pit he apologised for not sending me a paddock pass and I explained that I had one from Ken. I was keen to see the new 020 Tyrrells, which were designed by George Ryton with Harvey Postlethwaite. They were equipped with V10 Mugen Honda engines and had Braun sponsorship. Jean Alesi had left Tyrrell to join Ferrari, which was entirely understandable, but fortunately the talented Stefano Modena had taken his place in the team from Ockham. Jean Alesi called at the Tyrrell motor home at midday for a chat with Ken and Norah, as he would do most years. During lunch Ken came around to each table with a collecting tin for a charity saying, "that must be what they mean when they say there's no such thing as a free lunch!" Walking back to the pits after lunch, I perhaps unwisely asked Stefano's wife if she was anxious when her husband was racing but Norah quickly interjected "we don't talk about that." The second Tyrrell was driven by Satoru Nakajima but both cars were disappointing because, with the heavier engines and transverse gearboxes, they were inclined to be unbalanced and difficult to manage. Harvey Postlethwaite confessed that he had not been able to give sufficient time to developing the cars.

Such were the resources that McLaren had at their disposal that Ron Dennis had five cars at Silverstone with variants of the latest V12 Honda engine for Senna and Berger. There were three of the latest 643 Ferraris for Prost and Alesi, the last of which only being completed during the course of the two practice days. The official practice on Friday had to be suspended for 20 minutes to clear the track of oil dropped from Berger's McLaren Honda, but Nigel was fastest and the McLarens second and third. On Saturday there was a magnificent dual for pole between Nigel Mansell and Ayrton Senna, which Nigel won. Stefano Modena was 10th and Satoru Nakajima 15th.

Nigel Mansell was also fastest in the warm up and so his fans, who were assembled in great numbers, were confident that this would be a race to tell their grandchildren about.

The race: 59 laps of the 3.247 mile circuit

It was a hot summer's day for the race and at the start it was Senna who was first into Copse. Uncharacteristically, Mansell was a split second slower off the mark and then had to cope with some unwanted wheel spin but 'Red Five' was soon in front as his power advantage took him past the McLaren Honda along Hanger Straight. Patrese's Williams Renault and Berger's McLaren Honda touched at Copse and, as a result, Mansell's team mate dropped back to sixth place. Moreno's Benetton Ford came up from seventh to third place after a brilliant start but then slipped back through the field again behind the main contenders. Mansell proceeded to draw away in magnificent style from Senna while a crocodile formed behind Berger's McLaren Honda. The Ferraris of Prost and Alesi were next up but, when Alesi got ahead of his team mate and closed on Berger, touching Berger's McLaren Honda in his enthusiasm but fortunately without mishap. Oil spraying from Alesi's car clouded Prost's visor causing him to spin and drop to sixth place. Capelli missed a gear and spun out of the race. Such was Mansell's lead when he came in for a new set of tyres that there was no need for his pit crew to hurry and, afterwards, he continued to stretch the distance between himself and his pursuer as Senna could do nothing about it. Alesi retired after making contact with Suzuki's Lola Hart and de Cesaris had a massive accident with his Jordan Ford, fortunately without serious injury to himself. Stefano Modena was going well in sixth place in the Tyrrell Mugen Honda but eventually lost that place to Piquet. The cheering crowd was unaware of the fact that Mansell was nursing a fragile gearbox in the closing laps of the race but he made it safely to the finish a clear winner. When he coasted round again after the finish Ayrton Senna was sitting on the side pod of his car having run out of fuel.

Eddie Jordan chatting in the Jordan pits.

Andrea de Cesaris, a member of the Jordan team in 1991.

The striking colours and lines of the Jordan Fords.

Above: The 020 Tyrrell Ford.

Nigel Mansell's car being pushed back into his pit.

A view along the pit lane at lunch time.

Satoru Nakajima waiting in his car.

Stefano Modena about to
don his helmet. He would
be 10th in practice and 7th
in the race.

Ready for the off.

Stefano drives back...

...and his car is pushed back
into the garage.

Satoru Nakajima's car being
reversed as he sits at the
wheel.

THE 1992 BRITISH GRAND PRIX

SILVERSTONE JULY 10 11 12

"They love him and he loves them" –
Murray Walker

I APPROACHED SILVERSTONE on the Friday with good reason to be confident regarding Nigel Mansell's prospects as he had already won six of the first eight races in 1992 with his Williams Renault. I was rather less sure about how the latest Tyrrells would fare. The 020B Tyrrells, for which Mike Couglan was responsible, were powered by the compact V10 Ilmor engines and were to be driven by Olivier Grouillard and Andrea de Cesaris, who were both excellent drivers but neither would have claimed to be of the calibre of a Mansell or a Senna. In addition, Braun had withdrawn its sponsorship, and I ventured to suggest to Ken that he might offer one of the top drivers a really mind boggling salary and then, armed with his acceptance, approach a wealthy sponsor. He gently told me that it didn't work that way! Olivier Grouillard had problems with his gearbox and spun on Friday afternoon while Andrea de Cesaris was unhappy with the handling of his car. Andrea was 18th and Olivier 20th in the final practice.

Nigel Mansell was driving superbly and on the limit. He was fastest on both Friday and Saturday and thus secured pole position on the grid, while his team mate Riccardo Patrese shared the front row. Behind them were Ayrton Senna's McLaren Honda and Michael Schumacher's Benetton Ford. The last place at the very back was occupied by Damon Hill, driving an uncompetitive Brabham Judd in his first Grand Prix. The practice was shortened on Saturday after Eric Comas' Ligier Renault had rammed Riccardo Patrese's Williams Renault, writing off both cars.

The race: 59 laps of the 3.247 mile circuit

Wheel spin delayed Mansell fractionally at the start on Sunday and Patrese snatched a brief lead into Copse, but 'Red Five' soon passed and it was never challenged again. The Williams Renault was running beautifully and, with Mansell at the top of his form, it extended its lead steadily until its driver seemed content to hold it at about twenty seconds. Behind the two Williams Renaults, Brundle was having a brilliant race in his Benetton Ford ahead of Senna's McLaren Honda, Schumacher's Benetton Ford, and Herbert's Lotus Ford. While Mansell continued on his way, de Cesaris came in with a puncture on lap 23 after making contact with Modena's Jordan Yamaha and he subsequently retired. The main interest in the race centred upon the dual between those old rivals from Formula 3, Senna and Brundle, and

Results
1. **Mansell** Williams FW14B
   Renault V10
2. **Patrese** Williams FW14B
   Renault V10
3. **Brundle** Benetton B192
   Ford HB V8
4. **Schumacher** Benetton
   B192 Ford HB V8
5. **Berger** McLaren
   MP4 Honda V12
6. **Hakkinen** Lotus 107
   Ford HB V8
7. **Alboreto** Footwork
   FA13 Mugen V10
8. **Comas** Ligier JS37
   Renault V10
9. **Capelli** Ferrari F92A V12
10. **Boutsen** Ligier JS37
    Renault V10
11. **Grouillard** Tyrrell 020B
    Ilmor V10
12. **Suzuki** Footwork
    FA13 Mugen V10
13. **Lehto** BMS Dallara
    B192 Ferrari V12
14. **Tarquini** Fondmetal
    GR02 Ford HB V8
15. **Martini** BMS
    Dallara B192 Ferrari V12
16. **Hill** Brabham
    BT60B Judd V10
17. **Morbidelli** Minardi
    M192 Lamborghini V12

Failed to finish
Senna McLaren
MP4 Honda V12
De Cesaris Tyrrell 020B
Ilmor V10
Alesi Ferrari F92A V12
Modena Jordan 192
Yamaha V12
Gugelmin Jordan 192
Yamaha V12
Gachot Venturi LC92
Lamborghini V12
Herbert Lotus 197 Ford
HB V8
Wendlinger March
CG911 Ilmor V10
Katayama Venturi LC92
Lamborghini V12

Winner's average speed
143.109 mph

the two were side by side on lap 26. Mansell pitted for tyres on lap 30 without undue hurry, being stationary for a whole 12 seconds and still 8 seconds ahead of Patrese. On lap 31 Herbert retired with an inoperable gearbox having run in sixth place in his Lotus Ford while closing on the cars ahead of him. With typical understatement he said, "We were making progress all the time but were stuck in gear at the end – a bit of a shame." Schumacher came into the pits on lap 33 for tyres, having flat-spotted his first set in the course of his tussle with Senna and Brundle, while Mansell proceeded to delight the crowd, continually lowering the lap record and drawing the comment from Murray Walker, "they love him and he loves them". The dual between Brundle and Senna was resolved when Senna's gearbox failed on lap 52. Crowds swarmed on to the track as Mansell entered the finishing straight to win. They seemed to have forgotten that there would be cars following him at speed, and it was a miracle that no one was killed and only one injured, but the question of crowd control was the subject of serious discussion after the race. Mansell held the Union Jack aloft as he drove around the circuit to a standing ovation and he took his place on the podium with Patrese and Brundle to even more rapturous applause. Damon Hill, whose time was yet to come, finished 16th. Through this win, the seventh in a row, Mansell had exceeded Jackie Stewart's record to become the most successful British driver in Formula 1.

At the end of the Season Nigel Mansell emerged as the World Champion with 108 points compared to the 56 points of Riccardo Patrese who came second. In 1992, in addition to the British Grand Prix, he won the Grands Prix of South Africa, Mexico, Brazil, Spain, San Marino, France, Germany, and Portugal.

Views of the 020B Tyrrell with its Ilmor engine exposed, and of Andrea de Cesaris preparing to do a few laps in it.

Above: The graceful curves of the 1993 Tyrrell Ilmor.

Left: The Tyrrell motor home.

Below: Nigel Mansell's Williams Renault. Fastest in practice and winner of the race.

Close up of the great Ayrton
Senna who was 3rd in
practice but retired on lap
52 with gearbox trouble.
Tragically, he died at Imola
the next year.

Martin Brundle in his
Benetton Ford which was
6th in practice and finished
in 3rd place in the race.

Michael Schumacher's first
appearance at Silverstone,
driving his Benetton Ford, he
was 4th in practice, and
finished 4th in the race.

Mika Hakkinen was 9th in
practice in his Lotus Ford and
finished 6th in the race.

THE 1993 BRITISH GRAND PRIX

SILVERSTONE JULY 9 10 11

"50 for Prost" – Motor Sport

WHILE NIGEL MANSELL was engaged in winning the Indycar Series in America with the Newman Haas team, the Silverstone crowd was rooting for Damon Hill who drove the Williams Renault in his place. Could Damon win what was for British drivers the most important race in the calendar, the one which had always eluded his father, Graham? The ex Williams test driver had already secured four second places in 1993, presumably following team orders and deferring to Alain Prost. The question was asked would Frank Williams would allow him to make a real race of it with his team mate?

The Mike Cooglan designed 021 Tyrrell Yamahas were to be driven by Uyko Katayama and Andrea de Cesaris and Ken professed to be quietly confident about their prospects. He said that the Yamaha engine was as light as the previous year's Ilmor and that the car and its engine were exceptionally well matched. He joked that what he really wanted was to have Ayrton Senna drive one of his cars because he was one of the all time greats. I naively suggested to Ken the possibility of introducing adjustable wings which could be linked to the accelerators of the cars to give them maximum speed on the straights and maximum down force on the bends. He promised to send me a copy of the official Formula 1 regulations and when it arrived, inches thick I found of course that it excluded my suggestion. I was amazed to discover how minutely the design of Formula 1 cars was defined by the rules. What a contrast to the Grand Prix formula in 1934 which merely stipulated that the cars should weigh no more than 750 kg and be at least 850 cm wide! Due to the sponsorship of a cigarette manufacturer, packets of cigarettes were freely available on every table in the Tyrrell motor home but I didn't see any being smoked.

In the course of an extremely wet Friday Katayama was seventh fastest in the new Tyrrell Yamaha. However all eyes on Saturday were on the two Williams Renaults and Alain Prost just managed to better Damon Hill's time in the dying seconds of final practice. Michael Schumacher's Benetton Ford and Ayrton Senna's McLaren Ford were third and fourth. Of the Tyrrell Yamaha drivers, Andrea de Cesaris was 21st and Ukyo Katayama, having chosen the 020C car, 22nd.

The race: 59 laps of the 3.25 mile circuit

On Sunday afternoon Hill made a tremendous start and, in taking the lead, proceeded to open up a gap between himself and Senna's McLaren Ford. Prost, who had been slow off the line with wheel spin, was third while Schumacher was fourth and Brundle's Ligier Renault fifth. On lap 7 Prost went past Senna and he was followed through by Schumacher on lap 11. After this Prost steadily carved into Hill's lead of 8 seconds, although Hill proved that he was equally able to establish fastest laps. Prost stopped routinely for 8.02 seconds on lap 29 and Hill was in for 7.61 seconds on lap 30 but, after a fast out lap

1993 JULY 11th

BRITISH GRAND PRIX

Failed to qualify
M. Alboreto Lola Ferrari

Results
1. **Prost** Williams FWI5C
   Renault V10
2. **Schumacher** Benetton
   B193B Ford HB V8
3. **Patrese** Benetton
   B193B Ford HB V8
4. **Herbert** Lotus 107B
   Ford HB V8
5. **Senna** McLaren
   MP4 Ford HB V8
6. **Warwick** Footwork
   FA14 Mugen V10
7. **Blundell** Ligier JS39
   Renault V10
8. **Lehto** Sauber C12
   Ilmor V10
9. **Alesi** Ferrari F93A V12
10. **Barrichello** Jordan 193
    Hart V10
11. **Alliot** Larrousse
    LH93 Lamborghini V12
12. **Fittipaldi** Minardi
    M193 Ford HB V8
13. **Katayama** Tyrrell 020C
    Yamaha V10
14. **Brundle** Ligier JS39
    Renault V10

Not Classified
De Cesaris Tyrrell 021
   Yamaha V10

Failed to finish
Hill Williams FW15C
   Renault V10
Zanardi Lotus 107B
   Ford HB V8
Boutsen Jordan 193 Hart
   V10
Badoer Lola T93 Ferrari V12
Martini Minardi M193
   Ford HB V8
Wendlinger Sauber C12
   Ilmor V10
Berger Ferrari F93A V12
Suzuki Footwork FA14
   Mugen V10
Andretti McLaren MP4
   Ford HB V8
Comas Larrousse LH 93
   Lamborghini V12

Winner's average speed
134.235 mph

by Prost, Hill's lead was down to 3 seconds. The two Williams Renaults were racing in close formation when the Cosworth Ford Escort safety car was deployed, slowing everyone down. This was so that Badoer's Lola Ferrari could be retrieved from the grass near Woodcote Corner and opposite the pits, although some argued that it could have been quite safely left there undisturbed. It was even suggested that the safety car had been brought out merely to close the field up to make the race more exciting. That was hardly necessary and when normal racing was resumed on lap 40 the two Williams Renaults were circulating again in close formation although Schumacher had now been brought in touch with them. Hill, pulling out all the stops, registered the fastest lap of the race to put more distance between himself and his pursuer. Then, on lap 42 smoke and flames were emitted from Hill's engine and his race was over. The British Grand Prix had eluded the Hills again. For once the normally reliable Renault engine had let its driver down. This left Prost comfortably in the lead but, as he eased off, Schumacher began to gain on him until he was only 5 seconds behind. Prost responded to render his position quite safe and, with the race finishing in that order, Prost, scored his fiftieth win. He was almost apologetic when he stood on the podium in the place that everyone had hoped would have been occupied by Hill and generously said that Damon had deserved the win. It was good to see Herbert bringing his Lotus Ford home in fourth place. Senna stopped out of fuel on the last lap having been deceived by a faulty gauge, but he had still earned fifth place.

The Tyrrell Yamaha of Katayama was thirteenth and de Cesaris was still running at the end but sixteen laps behind the winner.

Andrea de Cesaris deep in thought while sitting in the 021 Tyrrell Yamaha...

...and ready to go.

021 with the monitor which kept Andrea informed of the up-to-the-minute lap times of all the other drivers.

Ukyo Katayama in his 021 Tyrrell Yamaha. He was 22nd in practice and finished 13th in the race.

Ken keeping a close eye on his team.

Damon Hill's Williams Renault in which he was second fastest in practice and led the race until his engine failed on lap 41.

Luca Badoer in his Lola Ferrari. He was 25th in practice and retired on lap 32 with an electrical failure.

The colours of Johnny Herbert's Lotus Ford are reflected in the rain-soaked pit lane. He was 7th in practice and finished in 4th place in the race.

Reflections, this time of
Ayrton Senna's McLaren Ford.
He was 4th in practice and
finished 5th in spite of running
out of fuel.

Fastening everything down on
Derek Warwick's Footwork
Mugen from the Arrows
stable. He was 8th in practice
and came 6th in the race.

Aguri Suzuki's Footwork
Mugen being reversed into its
pit. 10th in practice, he retired
on lap 8 after a spin.

THE 1994 BRITISH GRAND PRIX

SILVERSTONE JULY 8 9 10

"Hill stakes his claim" – *Motor Sport*

AYRTON SENNA HAD DIED at Imola on 1 May and his death was still on everyone's mind at Silverstone. Stirling Moss wrote to me, "It certainly was a terrible loss when Ayrton was killed. It is made even more tragic when you think how great he was and the fact that it was probably a mechanical failure and not an error on his part." Prince Rainier created a special tribute to the Brazilian driver in his Motor Museum at Monaco.

Refuelling had been reintroduced at the beginning of the 1994 Season and this meant that the teams had to calculate the relative advantages of one or two stop strategies as it increased the likelihood of gaining or losing places through pit stops.

The drivers for the 022 Tyrrell Yamahas were Ukyo Katayama and Mark Blundell. The Press was taking a great interest in Katayama and it was suggested that he might become the first Japanese driver to win the World Championship. Everyone was in a buoyant mood in the Tyrrell pits on Friday and watched the lap times of all the cars on the monitor screens during practice. As soon as it had ended, Ken gave me the "First Timed Session Classification" of the FIA hot off the press. It showed that Ukyo had been third fastest in practice and that Mark, whose car had suffered from a misfire, was eighth.

The famous band leader Chris Barber was a fellow guest in the Tyrrell motor home and he reminded Ken over lunch that he had promised to put on a concert to celebrate Tyrrell's next Grand Prix win. A good humoured discussion followed in which it was established that only the Albert Hall would do, and it was left undecided who would pay for it. Ken had brought to the motor home a portrait I had painted of him which he showed to everyone, and this led to my offering to paint one of the famous band leader too.

Damon Hill had already won the Spanish Grand Prix in 1994 with his Williams Renault and the competition between him and Michael Schumacher's Benetton Ford had become intense. On Friday Damon's suspension collapsed but on Saturday, when it really mattered, he beat his rival by the narrowest of margins to take pole position.

The race: 60 laps of the 3.21 mile circuit.
There had to be two formation laps as Coulthard stalled the Renault engine of his Williams on the line. Schumacher played mind games with Hill, momentarily overtaking him both times in clear violation of the rules. Undaunted, Hill made a magnificent start and had a full second lead on Schumacher by the

Failed to qualify
B. Gachot Pacific Ilmor
P. Belmondo Pacific Ilmor

Results
1. **Hill** Williams FW16
   Renault V10
2. **Schumacher** Benetton
   B194 Ford Zetec-R V8
3. **Alesi** Ferrari 412 V12
4. **Hakkinen** McLaren MP4
   Peugeot V10
5. **Barrachello** Jordan 194
   Hart V10
6. **Coulthard** Williams FW16
   Renault V10
7. **Katayama** Tyrrell 022
   Yamaha V10
8. **Frentzen** Sauber C13
   Mercedes V10
9. **Verstappen** Benetton
   B194 Ford Zetec-R V8
10. **Fittipaldi** Footwork FA15
    Ford HB V8
11. **Martini** Minardi M194
    Ford HB V8
12. **Herbert** Lotus 109
    Mugen Honda V10
13. **Panis** Ligier JS39B
    Renault V10
14. **Bernard** Ligier JS39B
    Renault V10
15. **Beretta** Larrousse HL94
    Ford HB V8
16. **Brabham** Simtek S941
    Ford HB V8
17. **Gounon** Simtek S941
    Ford HB V8

Failed to finish
Alboreto Minardi M194
   Ford HB V8
Berger Ferrari 412 V12
Blundell Tyrrell 022
   Yamaha V10
Comas Larrousse LH94
   Ford HB V8
De Cesaris Sauber C13
   Mercedes V10
Morbidelli Footwork FA15
   Ford HB V8
Zanardi Lotus 109 Mugen
   Honda V10
Brundle McLaren MP4
   Peugeot V10
Irvine Jordan 194 Hart V10

Winner's average speed
125.61 mph.

end of the first lap. Further down the grid both Irvine's Jordan Hart and Brundle's McLaren Peugeot blew up before their race had begun and Coulthard, trying too hard to make up places, spun on the first lap. Behind the leading pair were Berger's Ferrari, Barrichello's Jordan Hart and Alesi's Ferrari. Katayama was 8th, Herbert 14th and Blundell 15th. As Hill and Schumacher left the rest of the field behind, Schumacher was penalised by the officials for his misdemeanours before the start of the race and, after much heated discussion in the pit lane, eventually came in for his stop-go penalty. Before that, Hill stopped on lap 15 and Schumacher on lap 17, and this resulted in Berger leading the race until he too had a pit stop, leaving Hill in second place just behind Schumacher. When Schumacher served his stop-go penalty on lap 27 Hill was handed a lead over him of 29 seconds. As the race wore on it was Berger, Barrichello and Alesi who followed the leading pair and Katayama was up to seventh place. Blundell had a disastrous race in the second Tyrrell Yamaha because, having swerved to avoid the exploding engine of Brundle's McLaren Peugeot, his throttle jammed and his gearbox malfunctioned all in the same moment and he was forced to retire on lap 20. Higher up the field, Barichello overtook Berger to claim third place behind Hill and Schumacher until his scheduled pit stop on lap 41 dropped him to fifth. After this, Berger had Alesi and Hakkinen ahead of him with Frentzen's Sauber Mercedes immediately behind. Coulthard had made good progress after his unpromising start in the second Williams Renault and closed on Hakkinen after overtaking Frentzen, but Hill, now 16 seconds ahead of Schumacher, lapped his team mate on lap 51. Coulthard managed to unlap himself but then, becoming stuck in sixth gear, he was overtaken by Hill once more. Schumacher could make no impression on Hill as he was having gear selection problems and had flat-spotted his tyres. As the race neared its end there was some confusion as to whether Hill was on his last lap or whether he had a further lap to go. The crowd had no doubt about it and cheered him all the way round the circuit but, playing safe, he crossed the line at high speed. Thus a Hill won the British Grand Prix at last and Schumacher, who also experienced problems with his gearbox in the latter half of the race, finished 19 seconds behind him in second place. Katayama was seventh and David Brabham, son of Sir Jack Brabham, was sixteenth in a Simtek Ford. Princess Diana awarded the trophy to Damon Hill. Michael Schumacher later had his second place disallowed because of his infringement of the rules.

Williams making an impact in the paddock.

Benetton adding a splash of colour.

Mark Blundell who was 9th in practice in his 022 Tyrrell Yamaha and retired on lap 20 with gearbox trouble.

Mark keeping an eye on the opposition.

Mark Blundell preparing to go
out on to the circuit.

Mark checking lap times back
in the pits.

Returning to the pits after a
practice session.

Above: Ukyo Katayama's Tyrrell Yamaha awaiting its driver and its wheels.

Below: Katayama in his car and watching his monitor.

Above: Damon Hill's William's Renault before he gained pole position for the race.

Below: Damon Hill drives down the pit lane making for the circuit.

Gerhard Berger's Ferrari being sorted in the pits. 3rd in practice, he retired with engine trouble on lap 32 of the race.

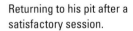

Berger setting out to record a fast lap.

Returning to his pit after a satisfactory session.

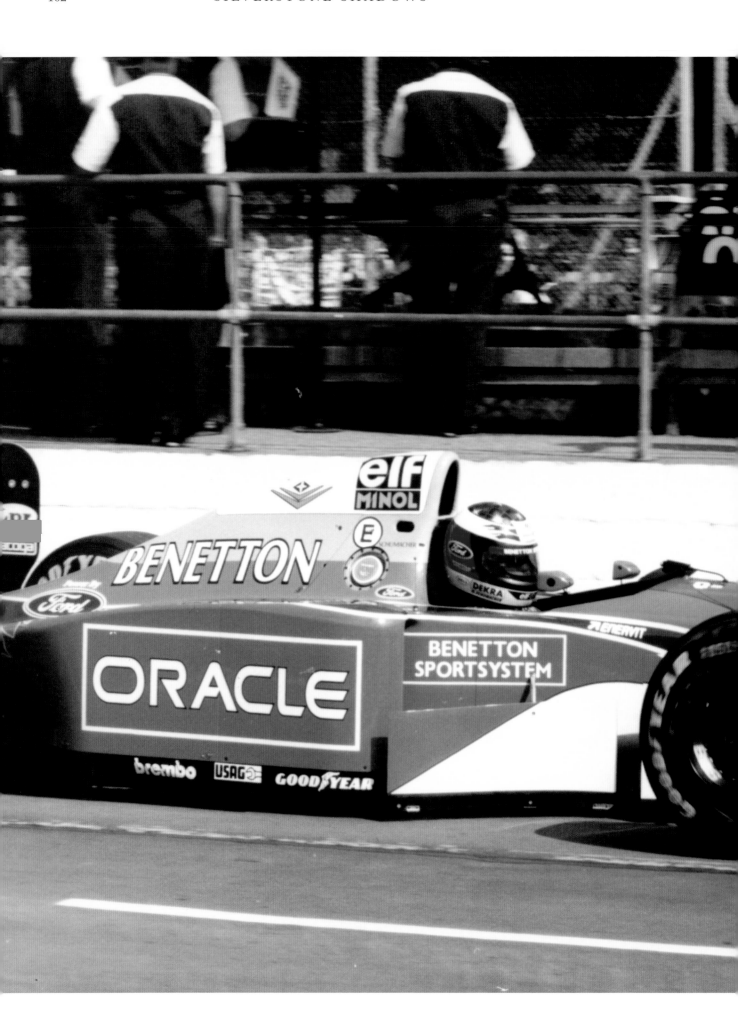

Michael Schumacher setting off down the pit lane.

Schumacher's car being
polished yet again. Second in
practice, his second place in
the race was disallowed.

Eddie Jordan relaxing over
lunch.

The author and famous Band Leader Chris Barber took turns to photograph each other with Ken Tyrrell after lunch in the Tyrrell motor home.

Frank Williams in a lighter moment.

Ron Dennis, the head of
McLaren, in a hurry.

Team Manager Rupert
Manwaring with Ken Tyrrell.

From left to right: Dr. Harvey
Postlethwaite, Jean Claude
Migeot, Mike Gascoyne,
Rupert Manwaring, Ken
Tyrrell and Simon.

THE 1995 BRITISH GRAND PRIX

SILVERSTONE JULY 14 15 16

"Johnny wins!" – Autosport

BRITISH ENTHUSIASTS CAME TO Silverstone in 1995 hoping to see Damon Hill win the British Grand Prix for the second year running in his Williams Renault.

The new regulations had reduced the engine size from 3.5 to 3 litres, and things looked good for the 023 Tyrrell Yamahas which had the financial backing of Nokia, and Ukyo Katayama had been joined by his promising new team mate Mika Salo.

The first thing I always did when I arrived at the circuit was to buy a programme and on this occasion both Ukyo and Mika signed it together with Ken and Norah. I was highly indignant when Mika's practice times on Friday were disallowed because he had missed a red light instructing him to stop at the weighbridge for a spot check, but Ken was surprisingly relaxed about it all. When I suggested that he should have been given prior warning of the check, he roared with laughter and said "How green can you get!" Ken was not always laid back but, while harsh words might be spoken, for example, when he believed that his drivers moved over too readily in being lapped, his good humour was soon restored and his famous guffaw heard in the motor home again. Mika was fourth fastest on Saturday, but only 23rd on the grid as heavy rain meant that no fast times were possible that day. Katayama was 14th.

Damon Hill was fastest both on Friday and Saturday but there was little action for the crowd to see on the second day of practice as it was clear that Friday's times could not be bettered. It was almost inevitable that Michael Schumacher's Benetton Renault was next to Damon Hill's Williams Renault. Behind them were David Coulthard's Williams Renault, Gerhard Berger's Ferrari and Johnny Herbert's Benetton Renault.

The race: 61 laps of the 3.14 mile circuit

Hill made a flawless start from pole and proceeded to gain a second a lap from Alesi's Ferrari, which had shot up from the third row to take second place from Schumacher at Copse. Panis and Barrichello were given stop-go penalties for jumping the start. Coulthard dropped back from fourth to ninth place when he made his pit stop on lap 17 and Alesi was back to seventh place after his stop the following lap. This at last let Schumacher, who had been held up behind the Ferrari, into second place and, having progressively reduced the deficit, he took the lead when Hill had his first pit stop on lap 22. Hill was stationary for 11 seconds and rejoined the circuit a full nine seconds down. He was to make two fuel stops to Schumacher's one and he regained the lead when the Benetton Renault stopped on lap 31 for 13.4 seconds. This gave Hill, with another stop yet to make, 20 seconds on Schumacher who was followed by Herbert,

WORLD CHAMPIONSHIP '95
16th JULY

Results

1. **Herbert** Benetton B195
   Renault V10
2. **Alesi** Ferrari 412 T2 V12
3. **Coulthard** Williams FW17
   Renault V10
4. **Panis** Ligier JS41 Mugan
   Honda V10
5. **Blundell** McLaren MP4
   Mercedes V10
6. **Frentzen** Sauber C14
   Ford Zetec-R V8
7. **Martini** Minardi M195
   Ford ED V8
8. **Salo** Tyrrell 023
   Yamaha V10
9. **Boullion** Sauber C14
   Ford Zetec-R V8
10. **Badoer** Minardi M195
    Ford ED V8
11. **Barrachello** Jordan 195
    Peugeot V10
12. **Gachot** Pacific PR02
    Ford ED V8

Failed to finish
Moreno Forti FGP
   Ford ED V8
Schumacher Benetton
   B195 Renault V10
Hill Williams FW17
   Renault V10
Papis Footwork FA16
   Hart V8
Katayama Tyrrell 023
   Yamaha V10
Montermini Pacific PR02
   Ford ED V8
Hakkinen McLaren MP4
   Mercedes V10
Berger Ferrari 412 T2 V12
Brundle Ligier JS41
   Mugen Honda V10
Inoue Footwork FA16
   Hart V8
Diniz Forti FGP Ford ED V8
Irvine Jordan 195
   Peugeot V10

Winner's average speed
122.30 mph.

Alesi, Coulthard and Blundell in the second McLaren Mercedes. Coulthard overtook Herbert to take third place and Hill made his second pit stop on lap 41, surrendering his lead, which he had managed to extend to 27 seconds, to come out of the pit lane in second place again. Herbert regained his third place when it was Coulthard's turn to stop. On fresh tyres Hill steadily closed on Schumacher's Benetton Renault until he was right behind it on lap 46 and he attempted to pass. Schumacher had taken a wide line into Priory and Hill shot into the gap. Both cars were squeezed together and both, digging themselves into the gravel, were suddenly out of the race. Hill said afterwards that it was a "racing accident" while Michael saw it quite differently, and afterwards both drivers were reprimanded by the Stewards. On lap 49 Coulthard passed Herbert to take the lead so that the Williams versus Benetton battle continued with both teams' second drivers. This exciting and hard fought contest ended when Coulthard was given a stop-go penalty for having speeded in the pit lane when his automatic speed limiter failed. So it was that Herbert emerged the winner, sixteen seconds ahead of Alesi with Coulthard third. Salo was eighth while Katayama had retired on lap 20 with a sudden loss of power. Brundle had retired after a spin on lap 9 and Berger's race had ended when the front left hand wheel of his Ferrari became loose after a pit stop on lap 21. Having been disappointed by Hill's retirement, the crowd was delighted that the victory had gone to Herbert. Everyone remembered his massive crash at Brands Hatch in 1988 and his courageous battle to get back to fitness and into a racing car afterwards. His was an inherited win, but there was nothing new about that in motor racing, and, having been on hand to pick it up, no one was more deserving of it than Johnny Herbert.

Ken Tyrrell at work.

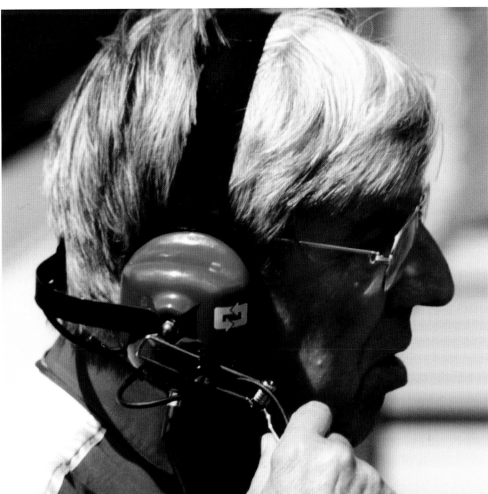

Jean Alesi chatting to Ken
and Norah.

Ken and Norah Tyrrell in their
motor home after lunch.

Tyrrell driver Mika Salo.

Ukyo Katayama was 14th in practice but retired on lap 22 with fuel starvation.

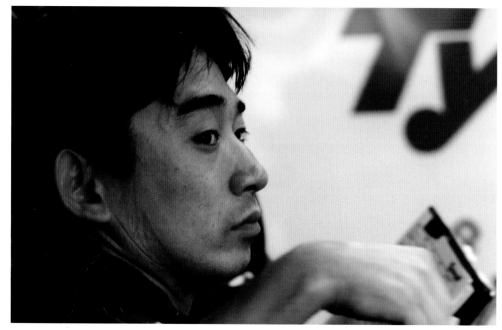

Mika Hakkinen's McLaren Mercedes was 8th in practice but retired with an electrical failure on lap 20.

Mika Salo sitting in his Tyrrell Yamaha after having had his Friday's time disallowed.

Ukyo Katayama returning to his pit.

Tyrrell number 3 being
reversed into the garage.

The Tyrrell men watching from
the pit wall.

Johnny Herbert being interviewed by BBC Five Live.

Overleaf: Johnny Herbert going out in the Benetton Ford with which he would win therace.

Johnny Herbert's personal
transport.

Scooters awaiting the Jordan
Peugeot drivers.

Gerhard Berger opted for a
yellow scooter.

Damon Hill was fastest in practice but tangled with Michael Schumacher on lap 46.

Mark Blundell's McLaren Mercedes, 10th in practice and 5th in the race.

Eddie Irvine's Jordan Peugeot. After qualifying in 7th place in practice he retired on the 2nd lap.

Above: The view from the footbridge of Mark Blundell's McLaren Mercedes being pushed back into its pit.

Below: Mark Blundell's car being passed by a Ligier Mugen in the pit lane.

THE 1996 BRITISH GRAND PRIX

SILVERSTONE JULY 12 13 14

"Jacques crashes Damon's party" – *Autosport*

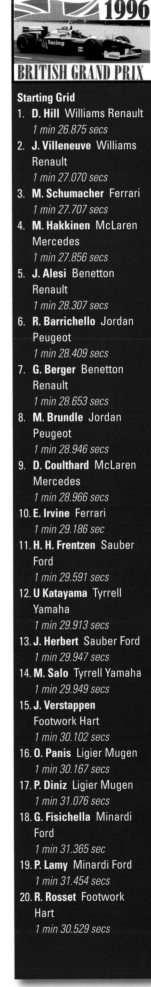

1996 WAS DAMON HILL'S YEAR. He had already won the Grand Prix of Australia, Brazil, Argentina, San Marino, Canada, and France. Surely he would win again at Silverstone?

The Tyrrells had Yamaha engines at Silverstone for the third year running in 1996. Ukyo Katayama's 024 Tyrrell Yamaha was twelfth fastest in practice. He said he was at last making a good recovery from the blow on the head he had sustained in Estoril the previous year. Importantly, Ukyo found that a new seating arrangement in his car was much more to his liking. His team mate Mika Salo was fourteenth. Both drivers said that the car handled well but they needed more power.

After lunch on the Friday Ken introduced me to Sir Jack Brabham who asked if he might borrow my pass for a few minutes. I couldn't help wondering if the stewards would believe me if, had I been challenged, I told them that Jack Brabham had borrowed it! I have to confess to being mildly relieved when he returned with it. Norah chatted to me about her family and said that Bob was taking more of the responsibility for the team off his father's shoulders. Ken introduced me to a well known motor racing artist and we had a good chat about the cars we had both seen at Goodwood in the 1950s. Of course we agreed that things were very different in the nineties and that the old cars with their open cockpits offered more scope for the artist than their modern counterparts. He told me that as a professional artist he was given very much less freedom of movement at race meetings than had been the case in earlier years.

Jacques Villeneuve was fastest on Friday being very much at home at Silverstone after doing many hours of testing there but, in what was to be his World Championship winning year, Damon Hill snatched pole position on Saturday, just 0.195 seconds ahead of his new Williams Renault team mate. Michael Schumacher was third, now driving a Ferrari, and next came Mika Hakkinen's McLaren Mercedes. Jean Alesi was unhappy with his Benetton Renault in fifth place, nearly one and a half seconds behind Hill, and Rubens Barrichello was next up in his Jordan Peugeot.

The race: 61 laps of the 3.152 mile circuit

90,000 people were there to watch Hill make a disastrous start, due in part to carrying a heavier fuel load, and it was the Williams Renault of Villeneuve which led Alesi, Hakkinen and Schumacher into the first bend. Back in fifth place Hill inevitably found that overtaking at Silverstone was to prove a massive problem but he at least gained one place when Schumacher's Ferrari retired on lap 3 with a leak in his hydraulic system, to much jeering and booing from an otherwise subdued crowd.

1996

BRITISH GRAND PRIX

Failed to qualify
A. Montermini Forti Ford
L. Badoer Forti Ford

Results
1. **Villeneuve** Williams
   FW18 Renault V10
2. **Berger** Benetton
   B196 Renault V10
3. **Hakkinen** McLaren
   MP4 Mercedes V10
4. **Barrichello** Jordan 196
   Peugeot V10
5. **Coulthard** McLaren
   MP4 Mercedes V10
6. **Brundle** Jordan 196
   Peugeot V10
7. **Salo** Tyrrell 024
   Yamaha V10
8. **Frentzen** Sauber C15
   Ford V10
9. **Herbert** Sauber C15
   Ford V10
10. **Verstappen** Footwork
    FA17 Hart V8
11. **Fisichella** Minardi
    M195B Ford V8

Failed to finish
Alesi Benetton B196
   Renault V10
Panis Ligier JS43
   Mugen Honda V10
Diniz Ligier JS43
   Mugen Honda V10
Hill Williams FW18
   Renault V10
Lamy Minardi M195B
   Ford V8
Rosset Footwork FA17
   Hart V8
Katayama Tyrrell 024
   Yamaha V10
Irvine Ferrari F310 V10
Schumacher Ferrari
   F310 V10

Winner's average speed
124.02 mph.

Irvine also retired on lap 5, after climbing to sixth place in the second Ferrari. All the while Villeneuve, whose car carried less fuel, drew steadily away from Alesi, Hakkinen and Hill, but it was Alesi's turn to lead when Villeneuve came in to the pits for his scheduled refuelling stop on lap 23. He was stationary for 9.5 seconds and slotted into fourth place afterwards, right behind Hill who had been held up for many laps by Hakkinen. Not long after this Hill sensed that something was odd about the handling of his car and on lap 26 his brakes suddenly failed. The cause of it all was that the nut had come loose on his left front wheel and the result was that he was sent into the gravel right in front of the crowded grandstand at Copse, his race over. Ironically Hakkinen stopped the following lap when it was just too late in the race for Hill to reap any advantage from it. With the two main protagonists eliminated from the contest the race had naturally become robbed of a lot of its interest. Villeneuve resumed his place at the head of the field on lap 31 when Alesi came into the pits and, on lap 44, Berger's Benetton gained second place when Alesi's identical car headed for the pits to retire with a failed wheel bearing. If it may be said that any Grand Prix can be dull, this was a dull one. The race resembled a procession with positions changing mainly through pit stops and retirements. Jacque Villeneuve richly deserved his first win at Silverstone but, long before the untimely end of his race, Damon Hill had bitterly regretted his poor start which had forced him to drive behind slower cars for lap after lap, unable to overtake them. Katayama had retired on lap 12 when his engine overheated and Salo finished in seventh place on a one stop strategy. A degree of suspense was introduced immediately after the race when Benetton claimed that the front wing end plates of the Williams Renaults failed to conform to the rules. They had been used all season having been accepted by Charlie Whiting of the FIA, and within four hours Villeneuve's place was officially ratified.

Damon Hill went on to win the Grands Prix of Germany and Japan, and the 1996 World Championship with 97 points. Jacques Villeneuve came second with 78 points.

Will it rain? Outside the McLaren motor home.

Far left: Damon Hill relaxing in the Williams motor home.

Left: Eddie Jordan in deep conversation with Bernie Ecclestone.

Michael Schumacher who would be World Champion no less than seven times.

Above: Eddie Irvine's Ferrari in the pits.

Below: Gerhard Berger's Benetton Renault.

Ukyo Katayama's 024 Tyrrell Yamaha.

A huddle in the Tyrrell pits including Chris White (the tallest figure), and Ukyo Katayama.

A Jordan Peugeot.

A Footwork Hart.

A Williams Renault.

Above: Gerhart Berger enjoying a joke with fellow Benetton driver Jean Alesi.

Below: Damon Hill in the Williams Renault with which he gained pole position but was forced to retire on lap 26 because of a loose wheel nut.

The Footwork pit crew in action.

Right: Jean Alesi with Alain Prost.

Far right: Sir Jack Brabham.

Michael Schumacher's Ferrari in the pit lane.

THE 1997 BRITISH GRAND PRIX

SILVERSTONE JULY 11 12 13

"Williams nets 100th GP victory" – *Autosport*

AFTER WINNING THE World Championship the previous year Damon Hill must have been surprised and disappointed to discover that his place in the Williams team had been given to Heinz-Harold Frentzen for the 1997 Season. Some rumours at Silverstone the previous year suggested that the German would be given Jacques Villeneuve's seat. As a result Damon drove an Arrows Yamaha in 1997 instead. He had no prospect of gaining a second World Championship with Arrows, whatever Tom Walkinshaw may have thought, but he astounded everyone when he qualified third fastest in practice for the Hungarian Grand Prix the following August, led the race and, in spite of a broken throttle cable, finished second to Jacques Villeneuve's Williams Renault.

The Stewart team was at Silverstone for the first time with the very latest Ford JD Zetec R V10 engine, having secured second place at Monaco with Rubens Barrichello. The team would win its first Grand Prix under the command of Sir Jackie and Paul Stewart before being taken over, first by Ford and then by Red Bull.

The 025 Tyrrell Fords had the ED V8 Ford Cosworth engines. The cars were designed by Harvey Postlethwaite and Mike Gascoyne, his Deputy Technical Director. Garry Thomas had been responsible for the gearboxes and Nigel Leaper for the manufacture of the bodies. Chris Cooney was their suspension engineer. The Michell Wind Tunnel at Southampton University had been vital in developing their aerodynamics and the cars had single central supports joining the wings to their raised noses. Mike Gascoyne said he would have liked more time with the test tunnel and a test team to manage it. At Silverstone engine failures frustrated both Mika Salo and Jos Verstappen so that they were 18th and 20th in practice.

Villeneuve and Frentzen were on the front row of the grid with their Williams Renaults and they had Hakkinen's McLaren Mercedes and Michael Schumacher's Ferrari immediately behind them. Michael Schumacher's brother Ralph was 5th in his Jordan Peugeot. Damon Hill was twelfth in his Arrows Yamaha but, remarkably, he was fastest of all comers in the warm up on Sunday morning.

The race: 59 laps of the 3.194 mile circuit

Frentzen stalled his engine on the starting line and so began his race at the back of the grid. All the cars consumed unplanned additional fuel in completing a second formation lap. Then Frentzen, too anxious to make up places at the start of the race, crashed into Verstappen's Tyrrell Ford and spun at Becketts so he was out after half a lap. The Tyrrell stopped for a new nose cone.

RAC British Grand Prix
Silverstone **1997**
10-11-12-13 July

Starting Grid

1. **J. Villeneuve** Williams Renault
   1 min 21.598 secs
2. **H H Frentzen** Williams Renault
   1 min 21.732 secs
3. **M. Hakkinen** McLaren Mercedes
   1 min 21.797 secs
4. **M. Schumacher** Ferrari
   1 min 21.977 secs
5. **R. Schumacher** Jordan Peugeot
   1 min 22.277 secs
6. **D. Coulthard** McLaren Mercedes
   1 min 22.279 secs
7. **E. Irvine** Ferrari
   1 min 22.342 secs
8. **A. Wurz** Benetton Renault
   1 min 22.344 secs
9. **J. Herbert** Sauber Petronas
   1 min 22.368 secs
10. **Fisichella** Jordan Peugeot
    1 min 22.371 secs
11. **J. Alesi** Benetton Renault
    1 min 22. 392 secs
12. **D. Hill** Arrows Yamaha
    1 min 23.271 secs
13. **J. Trulli** Prost Mugen
    1 min 23.366 secs
14. **S. Nakano** Prost Mugen
    1 min 23.887 secs
15. **J. Magnussen** Stewart Ford
    1 min 24.067 secs
16. **P. Diniz** Arrows Yamaha
    1 min 24.239 secs
17. **M. Salo** Tyrrell Ford
    1 min 24.478 secs
18. **U. Katayama** Minardi Hart
    1 min 24.553 secs
19. **J. Verstappen** Tyrrell Ford
    1 min 25.010 secs
20. **T. Marques** Minardi Hart
    1 min 25.151 secs
21. **R. Barrichello** Stewart Ford
    1 min 25.525 secs
22. **N. Fontana** Sauber Petronas
    Time disallowed

Results
1. **Villeneuve** Williams FW19 Renault V10
2. **Alesi** Benetton B197 Renault V10
3. **Wurz** Benetton B197 Renault V10
4. **Coulthard** McLaren MP4-12 Mercedes V10
5. **R. Schumacher** Jordan 197 Peugeot V10
6. **Hill** Arrows A18 Yamaha V10
7. **Fisichella** Jordan 197 Peugeot V10
8. **Trulli** Prost JS45 Mugen Honda V10
9. **Fontana** Sauber C16 Petronas V10
10. **Marques** Minardi M197 Hart V8
11. **Nakano** Prost JS45 Mugen Honda V10

Failed to finish
Hakkinen McLaren MP-12 Mercedes V10
Magnussen Stewart SF-1 Ford V10
Verstappen Tyrrell 025 Ford ED4 V8
Irvine Ferrari F310B V10
Salo Tyrrell 025 Ford ED4 V8
Herbert Sauber C16 Petronas V10
M. Schumacher Ferrari F310B V10
Barrichello Stewart SF-1 Ford V10
Diniz Arrows A18 Yamaha V10
Frentzen Williams FW19 Renault V10
Katayama Minardi JS45 Hart V8

Winner's average speed
128.445 mph.

At the front Villeneuve made an excellent start and led Michael Schumacher by a whisker from Coulthard and Hakkinen. That order was maintained with the first two cars drawing away from the rest until the safety car came out for Katayama's stricken Minardi Hart to be removed. Then, when racing was resumed in earnest, the order was Villeneuve, Schumacher, Coulthard and Hakkinen, but Villeneuve became aware that of the fact that something was wrong with the front corner of his car, yet managed to hold his position. Michael Schumacher stopped on lap 21 but retained his second place when he emerged from the pit lane. Then he found himself to be leading the race when Villeneuve came in on lap 22 and was delayed for 34 seconds in his pit. Villeneuve's problem proved to have been a loose wheel which perversely refused to be removed from the car during the pit stop. The order had thus become Schumacher, Coulthard and Hakkinen, with the leader well clear of his pursuers.

On lap 28 Hakkinen, who had been held up for many laps by Coulthard managed to pass the Scotsman when his brakes locked up. Coulthard dropped down to tenth place when he stopped for new tyres. Hakkinen also pitted three laps later and came out in eighth spot. At this stage Michael Schumacher was in front with a clear lead from the Benetton Renaults of Alesi and Wurz who held their positions until they too pitted, leaving Hakkinen second and Villeneuve third. Then Schumacher was suddenly removed from contention on lap 38 with a failed wheel bearing. This left Villeneuve, who had overtaken Hakkinen, in the lead once more, with Irvine, Hakkinen, Alesi, Wurz and Coulthard behind him in that order. Irvine retired on lap 44 with a broken half shaft and Villeneuve made his second pit stop on the same lap, falling back to second place, six seconds behind Hakkinen. The Williams driver proceeded to reduce the gap as Hakkinen's tyres were blistering and losing grip and the McLaren Mercedes stopped on lap 53 with a blown engine. Convinced that he could have held Villeneuve off to the end, Mika Hakkinen was bitterly disappointed, but it was Villeneuve who was in front when it mattered, followed by Alesi, Wurz, Coulthard, and Michael Schumacher's brother Ralf. Damon Hill was sixth in the Arrows Yamaha, thus scoring the team's first points to the acclaim of a loyal crowd.

Both Tyrrell Fords had retired with engine problems, as had the two the Stewart Fords. Mika Salo's car lasted until lap 44 and Jos Verstappen went just one lap further.

TYRRELL   RACING   ORGANISATION   LTD

Bryan

Tyrrell

Long Reach, Ockham, Woking, Surrey, England GU23 6PE
Telephone 01483 284955   Fax 01483 284892

Enclosed your Friday pass for Silverstone, I look forward to seeing you at lunch

Ken

WITH COMPLIMENTS

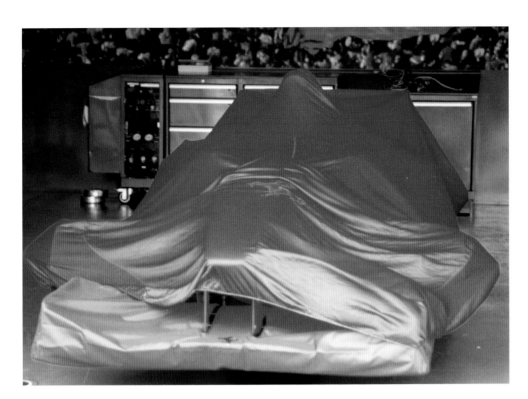

A Ferrari shrouded in mystery.

The mystery revealed.

The Benetton Renault to be
driven by Alexander Wurz.

Mika Hakkinen's McLaren
Mercedes.

The Arrows Yamaha.

Johnny Herbert's Sauber
Petronas.

One of the Jordan Peugeots.

A Prost Mugen Honda

Mika Salo's 025 Tyrrell Ford at close quarters.

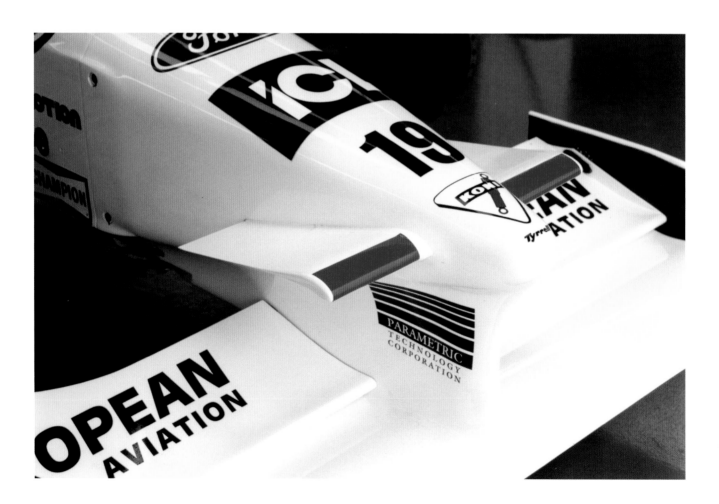

A mechanic working on a Tyrrell Ford during the lunch break.

Tyrrell driver Jos Verstappen whose Benetton was engulfed in flames while on a pit stop during the German Grand Prix in 1994.

Jos Verstappen about to put in
some more laps.

Mika Salo who would be 17th
in practice and retire with
engine trouble on lap 44.

Dr Harvey Postlethwaite
studying the lap times on the
monitor screen.

Above: Stewart Ford driver Rubens Barrichello. The photograph was signed later at Beaulieu by Sir Jackie Stewart.

Below: Rubens Barrichello venturing out in his Stewart Ford.

Eddie Irvine who was 7th in
practice but retired on lap 44
with transmission trouble.

Giancarlo Fisichella.

Damon Hill with the famous
colours of the London Rowing
Club.

Simon Taylor, the motor racing
journalist and broadcaster.